T0167149

YATUVAY
THE MANUAL

How to Perform
MIRACULOUS HEALING
Through
ENERGY MEDICINE

BY ADOLPHINA SHEPHARD

iUniverse, Inc.
New York   Bloomington

YATUVAY – The Manual
How to Perform Miraculous Healing Through Energy Medicine

Copyright © 2009 Adolphina Shephard

All rights reserved. No part of this book may be used or reproduced by any means,
graphic, electronic, or mechanical, including photocopying, recording, taping or by any
information storage retrieval system without the written permission of the publisher
except in the case of brief quotations embodied in critical articles and reviews.

The information, ideas, and suggestions in this book are not intended as a substitute for professional
medical advice. Before following any suggestions contained in this book, you should consult your personal
physician. Neither the author nor the publisher shall be liable or responsible for any loss or damage allegedly
arising as a consequence of your use or application of any information or suggestions in this book.

iUniverse books may be ordered through booksellers or by contacting:

iUniverse
1663 Liberty Drive
Bloomington, IN 47403
www.iuniverse.com
1-800-Authors (1-800-288-4677)

Because of the dynamic nature of the Internet, any Web addresses or links contained in
this book may have changed since publication and may no longer be valid. The views
expressed in this work are solely those of the author and do not necessarily reflect the views
of the publisher, and the publisher hereby disclaims any responsibility for them.

ISBN: 978-1-4401-3872-0 (pbk)
ISBN: 978-1-4401-3874-4 (cloth)
ISBN: 978-1-4401-3873-7 (ebk)

Library of Congress Control Number: 2009927160

Printed in the United States of America

iUniverse rev. date: 6/3/2009

Important Note

The information contained in this book is intended for education purposes only. If you are ill or have been injured, it is my hope that you will derive the benefit of the lesson that it was intended to teach you. However, it does not mean you should not support your body in the physical and seek medical attention.

The author, publisher and distributors of this work accept no responsibility for anyone misusing the potential empowering information and revelations in this book.

Any similarity to anyone living or dead is strictly coincidental.

Dedication

I dedicate this book in loving memory to my beloved and dearest mother, Momsy, who last year crossed to the other side.

I include my beloved pets, Schoochie and Sweet Pea, who filled my heart with joy and recently joined Momsy on the other side of the veil.

I love you all very much and wish for you all of the peace and the fullness of The Lord, God.

Special Thanks

I want to thank my darling husband, Steve, for all of his support, strength and help throughout these many years. Without his support on all levels of being, on our shared journey, whether on a physical, mental, emotional or spiritual basis, this book would not have been able to come into existence. Thank you, Steve, my love, for always being there for me and by my side.

I want to thank, Kathy, who has assisted greatly by taking much time and effort to assist in the editing of this book. Without her help, it would have been practically impossible to complete this book efficiently, and on a timely basis. Thank you, Kathy, for all of your efficiency, knowledge and support. Additionally, I want to thank, LuAnn, for all of her dedicated, timely assistance in proofreading this book.

I thank all of my spiritual family for all of your support though many difficult times, and for being there when I needed you. I also thank you for the many uplifting, joy-filled times, particularly, Debbie and Jerry, Patricia, Beverly, Charles and Susie, Victoria, Joseph, Miriam, Judy, Ed, Wendy, Mikey and Jamie, LuAnn, Kathy, Jan, and my loving cat, Tippy. If I have forgotten anyone, please forgive me and know that you too are very much appreciated.

I cannot forget my loving friend, Dr. Simon, who has not only given me great love, spiritual strength and knowledge, but has also shared the use of his office on many occasions for my classes and workshops.

Last, but certainly not least, I wish to thank God and The Company of Heaven for your guidance, support, wisdom, love, and for lighting the way on my path and journey. Thank you all. I love you from the bottom of my heart.

Introduction

Adolphina Shephard is an Intuitive, Pioneer, Etheric Surgeon, and experienced Metaphysician in the Field of Energy Medicine, who teaches a vast variety of techniques of Energy Medicine, through the Modality of YATUVAY. She has helped many achieve wellness who had no hope left of regaining their health, or experiencing happiness once again. She is a conduit for the Holy Trinity, in service to God to assist humanity, and receives new knowledge given to her in this manner. The Hebrews have a word for this, it is called Hashem, which means that the knowledge is given by God.

She is a gifted teacher and speaker on the *unknown truths or the higher reality.* Adolphina has always been a seeker and visionary having had many supernatural brushes with the unknown since early childhood. This lead her to study matters of spirituality and the supernatural her entire life.

Five years ago, the Ascended Master and Lord Jesus Christ, began working intensely with Adolphina through and with the Holy Spirit and the I AM THAT I AM to teach her Holy mysteries. There are many reasons that the information in this book is being released at this time. One reason, is so that everyone can have a straight forward, easy to read understanding of how Energy Medicine works. So that everyone may feel comfortable seeking and receiving Energy Medicine. Another reason this book was created, is to be a reference book for Energy Medicine Practitioners, enabling them to put all the pieces together, to formulate a cohesive plan for creating miraculous healings through Energy Medicine. Ultimately, all of the reasons are to assist humanity.

Additionally, this book details what it takes to become a highly skilled practitioner of Energy Medicine, for self-healing, friends and loved ones. Lastly, so that Adolphina may assist humanity in the healing and ascension of the human race. She has had to undergo many initiations, fiery trials and tests, before being allowed to release and teach these methods to humanity. She continues to receive ongoing training, healing and initiatory upgrades.

I would like to give you an example of what is meant by fiery trials and tests; One day Adolphina started experiencing severe chest pains, with pain radiating out to her jaw and arms. It felt like there was an elephant sitting on her chest. This resulted in being rushed to the hospital, where she was admitted to the hospital because it was apparent she was in the throes of a heart attack. Upon gathering her wits about what was happening, Adolphina was able to avert a major heart attack by her knowledge of Energy Medicine and by utilizing it on herself.

The doctors and nurses where baffled as to why they then could find no evidence of a heart attack, as it seemed apparent that this was what was occurring upon admittance. Upon her release from the hospital, Adolphina received a telephone call by her primary doctor, who wanted to see her, and how she was doing after this horrific experience. The next day, she went to see her doctor, who actually wanted to see her because she had received a very clear message for Adolphina from the Holy Spirit. Her doctor, whose name is not going to be revealed, keeps this great gift under wraps, to preserve her reputation in the medical community, who look at clairvoyance as something of a joke. The message was, *that this potential heart attack was the result of Adolphina not actively involved in the process of writing her first book, (Living With Spirit ~ Going Beyond The Physical), although she had been thinking about it. That she was not fulfilling what she came to do on Earth. It was made pretty clear, that this message was a step-up to the plate to fulfill her mission or else message. That this experience was a lesson for her.* These are the types of fiery trials that bring enlightenment. Who would have thought that something like a potential heart attack could be the result of not being on your spiritual path? It was definitely a big revelation and awakening for Adolphina.

Her interest in Energy Medicine initially occurred as a result of being in a car accident, leaving her with disabilities that traditional medicine could not remedy. Prior to having the car accident, Adolphina was a highly successful businesswoman in the corporate world of marketing and insurance. Having no desire to remain disabled, with a strong desire to be well again, led her on an amazing journey of self-healing and discovery. Thus, Adolphina, underwent many different forms of Complimentary and Alternative Holistic Therapies. In this process, learning a great deal about different forms of Energy Medicine in her quest to be well.

This self-healing journey piqued her interest and led her to Energy Medicine, where she studied various forms of Energy Medicine such as Laying-On-Of-The-Hands on a Christian Basis and Frequency Balancing, with Judy DiCanio. In addition, Adolphina went on to study Energy Medicine on a much larger basis, through the modality of Feng Shui, with Victoria Pendragon at the Metaforim. She was led to Feng Shui because Feng Shui deals with a larger aspect of Energy Medicine, in the form of property and the land. Few people know that their property or land can be at the root cause of any challenge that they may be experiencing.

Furthermore, Adolphina and her husband learned and practiced Professional Aura Photography. By taking, reviewing and analyzing hundreds of Aura Photographs, this enhanced her knowledge of The Electromagnetic Body, since Aura Photographs are like an X-Ray of the Electromagnetic Body.

Her first book, (*Living With Spirit, Going Beyond the Physical*), is a glimpse at the interaction of the physical and spiritual worlds as Adolphina experienced it. This new book, YATUVAY, is written in service to God, for the benefit of humanity, under the guidance of the Holy Trinity. This is so that humanity can live a glorious and joyous life by experiencing good health as God intended, when we were created.

Eventually, her knowledge and understanding of the Electromagnetic Body led to the development of YATUVAY, a Modality of forty-two different techniques that work by the principle of *The Power Of One*. Her new book, (*YATUVAY ~ The Manual, How To Create Miraculous Healings Through The Energy Medicine*), will be the go-to-book for Energy Medicine Practitioners, to assist them in putting all of the pieces together to create miraculous healing.

By having the reference material and the training given in this book, this will change the very face of medicine by teaching how *illness starts first in the Spiritual Bodies not the Physical Body.* This is where the root cause is, in the Spiritual Bodies. You will learn that there are actually four different bodies with many sub-systems, to a human body, not just the Physical Body.

These additional invisible Spiritual Bodies, when not in good shape affect the Physical Body, *as a consequence of a problem in the Spiritual Bodies.* You will learn how and why the body becomes ill through the Electromagnetic Body and the other bodies, and how to resolve these issues on a natural and permanent basis.

Additionally, many have no idea of the ramifications of their negative thoughts and attitudes, thereby creating their ill health. You will learn how negative thoughts and attitudes create illness, and the steps you need to know so that you can change these thought processes. This will change the way people will look at their thoughts, how they react to any given circumstances, and how it affects their bodies and life from reading this book. YATUVAY, The Modality, and this book, has been given by God, and written so that humanity may have a natural method of restoring and maintaining good health.

Adolphina currently resides in the state of New Jersey with her husband, Steve, of twenty-five years. She lectures extensively around the country at conferences, seminars and expos. Adolphina teaches monthly YATUVAY Workshops to those who are interested in holistic medicine, desiring a natural way to stay healthy and to Energy Medicine Practitioners, from the novice to the master, desiring to learn Advanced Energy Medicine Techniques.

Adolphina's goal is to spread YATUVAY globally via an Virtual-School to compliment this book, and by lecturing at colleges, seminars and conferences on this subject. This goal is in service to God, so that humanity's lives will improve on a physical, mental, emotional and spiritual basis with great joy, as you open the door to completely new thought, new knowledge and a new world. In the fulfillment of this goal, YATUVAY, will form a web of Light throughout the world, which will greatly assist with the coming galactic convergence in 2012.

Contents

CHAPTER I ~

Changing The Very Face of Medicine

The reason that this book will change the face of medicine is because, *the root cause of all illness exists in the Spiritual Bodies of man, not in the Physical Body. The challenges with the Physical Body are a consequence of what is occurring in the Spiritual Bodies. Therefore, in order for permanent healing to take place, the root cause in the Spiritual Bodies must be resolved.* There are four main Spiritual Bodies in the human body, with many sub-systems, that exist to create the whole. The four main Spiritual Bodies are, The Electromagnetic Body, The Mental Body, The Emotional Body, and The Physical Body. Do you remember a Bible verse, which is quoted from the New American Standard Bible that reads?

For even as the body is one, and yet has many members, and all the members of the body, though they are many, are one body, so also is Christ.

Corinthians I:12:

This verse is a very true statement! In traditional medicine, the focus is on the Physical Body, but that is not where *the root cause* exists! Unfortunately, the Physical Body receives all of the *miscreations that are created by the other Spiritual Bodies. Once we change the focus of where we are looking for the root cause to the Spiritual Bodies and fix them, much illness will be easily eliminated.* In the East, traditional medicine covers the body, mind, and the spirit. This is somewhat better. However, still missing is the Electromagnetic Body, and all of its many sub-systems, that work together to form a cohesive whole, with the main bodies of the Mental, Emotional and Physical. We will cover sub-system's further in Chapter 4.

There are a small percentage of people worldwide, who are called Light Workers, because they work with the Light or energy. I call these Light Workers, Energy Medicine Practitioners. This group of people is aware that the Electromagnetic Body exists as a consequence of working with energy. It is unfortunate that few know about the Electromagnetic Body other than Light Workers, because it is the Electromagnetic Body, which feeds the Physical Body *the very energy for life itself.* There is also the Mental Body, which creates our thoughts and consciousness. There is the Emotional Body, which *fans the flames and* is responsible for whatever the Mental Body has thought up or vice versa.

Further, we have many sub-systems that I will go into later, which include the Psychic Body, which tells us intuitively, when to do something or not to do something. In order to thrive instead of just survive; we must treat all of the bodies. You may wonder why I am at all concerned about the Psychic Body. The reason is that if the Psychic Body were fully working, then intuitively, we would know that wearing an electrical appliance on our belt next to our liver, colon, brain or ear all day, might disrupt our body's energy. This can cause all sorts of challenges, from potential brain tumors to colon or liver cancer.

Another reason is that for the average person, who is curious about Energy Medicine, I will teach them, a basic system, so that they do not have to participate in the so-called *death economy.* This is where a person who is ill, runs from one doctor to another, taking test after test, or taking five, ten or fifteen different medicines, which is *simply treating the symptom instead of fixing the root cause* until death occurs. This is why it is referred to as the *death economy.* The death economy is a trillion dollar industry where many people make their living off of you being sick. However, by you becoming informed by reading this book, can take charge of your own health. I will teach you how, through the natural method of healing through Energy Medicine without pain, pills or physical surgery.

We all know of someone who has never found a resolution for his or her illness, or why he or she feels so bad. This is because the resolution is in the Electromagnetic Body, not in the Physical Body. You will learn why a sick Electromagnetic Body is the root cause of many, if not most, illness that exists, and how Energy Medicine is not only curative, but also preventative medicine. Would you like to be as healthy as you possibly can be without drugs, needles or surgery? Would you like to restore your health? If so, this book is for you.

For the established Energy Medicine Practitioner, this book will be very helpful because it will allow you to formulate a cohesive plan to bring your clients back to wellness. The challenge that most Energy Medicine Practitioners run up against, is that they have learned different techniques piecemeal, and cannot see how to put all the pieces together to perform a cohesive miraculous healing. However, by utilizing this book, you will find it very easy to put all of the pieces together and this challenge will be resolved. In Chapter 7-The Manual, you will find that it weaves together all of the energetic techniques necessary to form a complete picture for the healing of the Electromagnetic Body. Additionally, *this book is a vehicle, where you will experience the expansion of your consciousness, leading to enlightenment.*

In this book, I will show you how Energy Medicine is the first step that you will take before making any serious medical decisions, such as surgery. You will see that you have the potential to go off medications, and restore good health for even chronic illnesses such as diabetes, chronic fatigue, asthma, thyroid problems, heart challenges, arteriosclerosis, liver and kidney problems, etc. Even cosmetic surgery for face-lifts, eyebrow lifts, jowl and neck lifts can be achieved with Energy Medicine.

I will teach you how Energy Medicine will cause you to thrive, instead of just survive, and how you can restore your health. Thereby, your joy, because without your health, you having nothing. With Energy Medicine, you will learn how to find the root cause of an illness, and how to correct it, so that health can be restored. Your very perception of how your body works will be forever changed. I will teach you how your thought processes affect your physical health. You will see how radionics, accidents, electromagnetic frequencies, and especially your negative thought processes are responsible for ill health.

I will teach you how to lose the *victim consciousness*, which is an attitude that says, *everything happens to poor me*, translating into bad health. I will then go on to show you how to repair and build your Electromagnetic Body. In Chapter 7, you will find *The Manual*, which will show you a list of common illnesses, and the necessary techniques, along with practical suggestions, that are necessary to perform miraculous healings through Energy Medicine. You will be able to simply look up a common illness in The Manual, find the probable cause and what is needed to restore wellness. Lastly, you will be shown what steps to take to experience continual wellness for yourself and others.

Additionally, according to the Philadelphia Inquirers Parade Magazine, dated October 19, 2008, it was reported, that by 2013, it is projected that there will be a shortage of over 60,000 doctors in the United States. I believe that this projected shortage will lead many people to Energy Medicine.

CHAPTER 2 ~

Just What Is The Problem?

The biggest challenge lies in the fact that most people cannot understand what they cannot see with the naked eye. The Electromagnetic Body is invisible to the naked eye, as well as the *other Spiritual Bodies of the Emotional, Mental, and the Sub-Systems* that work together to form a cohesive whole. Most people are limited to their five senses of hearing, sight, smell, taste and feel. If they cannot see it, feel it, smell it, or taste it, then they do not believe in it. Although there are some people who are gifted with psychic sight, and can see energy, most people cannot.

Another challenge with Energy Medicine is that, for the most part, people are unaware that these four bodies exist. This is because, with the exception of the Physical Body, these bodies exist but are physically and medically invisible. The Electromagnetic Body will not show up on an x-ray, a CAT scan or an MRI. It can, however, be captured with Aura Photography Technology, which utilizes a hand plate with tiny, metal probes, called Acuflow probes, that measure the electromagnetic charge of your body. In addition, a webcam will pick up additional features of the Electromagnetic Body that the naked eye cannot see. I do not understand how a webcam and, even sometimes, a regular camera can pick up esoteric images and beings. I have seen many oddities when using a webcam and a regular old camera, whether digital or not. Many times, if I see something extraordinary in a photo, I will scan it or download the picture onto the computer, where I can enlarge it and sharpen the picture to see what it is.

Nicola Tesla is one of the first known researchers of this technology, who photographed himself, using high voltage energy in 1891. The Soviet Union did further research in the 1960's. In 1970, Guy Coggins, who is the manufacturer of the Aura Camera equipment that I use, was fascinated by Kirlian Photography and computer technology. He brought his technical skills, his ability to see auras, and his desire to make alternative consciousness available for everyone, to develop the first Aura Camera. His equipment uses very low voltage energy instead of the higher voltage used by Kirlian Photography. Modern aura imagining tools can detect the presence of chakras, which are major energy centers that feed your body energy. It is possible to capture the seven primary chakras with an Aura Camera. However, only those gifted with clairvoyant sight can see Auras. Some people can sense or intuit the Aura.

Aura photography captures on paper what scientists' term *biofield* to describe the radiant energy that surrounds *all living things*. Aura Photography Systems use *biofeedback technology*. Then, the Aura equipment produces an electronic interpretation of what the Aura looks like. The biofeedback apparatus measures the electrical potential along the meridian points in the palm of the hand. This is done with a hand plate that you hold your hand on while the picture is taken. It then converts that information to an electrical frequency that displays this as colors and patterns. Many psychics can see aura frequencies. Their inner eye or third eye perceives these frequencies as colors. Guy did much research as well as corroborating with many psychics to ascertain that the colors were accurate. Guy himself has psychic sight, which greatly assisted him in this endeavor. He then went on to develop the equipment so that the colors seen by not only him, but also other psychics matched the colors in the human Aura.

By utilizing sophisticated hi-tech Aura Equipment, energy is measured in megahertz and manifested as a color because all color has a frequency. This is quantum physics in a simple form.

Quantum physics according to our friend, Webster's Dictionary, simply means:

1. Quantity or amount.

2. Very small, indivisible quantity of energy.

3. Sudden and significant.

In fact, only a small percentage of the population has knowledge of the Electromagnetic Body. There are over six and a half billion people on this planet, but there are only about fifteen million Energy Medicine Practitioners in various Alternative and Complementary Practices spread throughout the world. This is why there is a general lack of widespread public knowledge of the Electromagnetic Body. To add to the reason why there is a lack of public knowledge is because many of these techniques have been keep hidden by secret societies, and The Mystery Schools that few people know anything about. Additionally, in indigenous cultures, many of these teaching were passed down in an oral tradition and kept within their own cultures.

However, Energy Medicine has their roots in many ancient teachings from various parts of the world. For example, from Egypt came the Mystery Schools with various esoteric teachings, India gave us the Chakra System, from China came Acupuncture and the Meridian System. The Tibetan monks in the United States often hold Karma Clearings. Much of this esoteric knowledge goes back to the ancient World of Atlantis. We, in the western hemisphere of the United States, are only in the beginning stages of accepting these ancient mysteries and teachings. If we were to combine the western world's traditional medicine with Energy Medicine, we would see such an increase in vitality and health.

It is my belief that Energy Medicine will become a primary tool for preventative and curative medicine in the future, in compliment to traditional medicine. There are a few reasons for this belief. One of the main reasons according to the Philadelphia Inquirer's Parade Magazine, is that by 2013 there will be a projected shortage of over 60,000 medical doctors in the United States. People will have a tough time getting in to see a doctor. Next, we have the issue of the cost of medical insurance. Many people live without medical coverage and are looking for natural ways to stay healthy. Another reason is that we have many people looking for holistic alternatives to the traditional methods of surgery, chemotherapy and drugs. Further, the baby boomers are graying and I do not see how the traditional medical field can possibly accommodate such an enormous demographic of people, in medical facilities, hospitals and nursing homes. There may not even be enough doctors to take care of such an extremely large demographic of people who are going to need medical assistance, especially, with the projected shortage of medical doctors. Lastly, in recent years we have had a spate of tragedies around the world in the manner of floods, tsunamis, hurricanes, tornadoes, earthquakes, etc. Should a tragedy occur that a large city such as New York, including its hospitals were disabled, how will people help themselves and others who need assistance?

There are many different types of energy practitioners. Many people know about Acupuncture and that it works by inserting needles into the meridians. What most people are *unaware of is that these meridians are invisible*. Meridians are similar in nature to lymph or blood vessels except that what the meridians contain, instead of blood or lymph fluid, is invisible energy. The Meridian System is one of the Sub-Systems of the Electromagnetic Body. If a doctor were to cut you open, he would not be able to find the meridians. Only an experienced energy practitioner is able to see, feel, or sense the meridians.

A gifted Acupuncturist can feel where a blockage lies with their fingertips before they insert a needle into an Acuflow Point, in an attempt to stimulate and unblock a meridian, allowing energy to flow once again. By unblocking the flow of energy, the body once again can be fed the energy to heal itself. However, Acupuncturists are not trained in the methods I am about to expose you to.

You may wonder about the term, Metaphysician, and how it was coined. The Metaphysical Universal Ministries and Learning Center defines it this way:

Metaphysical ~ (Greek Origin) *beyond: in simple terms, beyond the five senses, intuition, and perception.*

Meta as stated in Webster's Dictionary means *Meta ~* prefixes meaning:
1. After or beyond as in metaphysics.
2. Change, as in metamorphosis.

Both of these definitions aptly apply to repairing the Electromagnetic Body.
Physics as stated in Webster's Dictionary means:

1. *Science of matter, motion, energy and force.*

Put *Meta, Physics,* together, and it becomes *Metaphysics.*

Metaphysics as stated in Webster's Dictionary means:
1. Branch of philosophy concerned with the ultimate nature of reality.

Philosophy as stated in Webster's Dictionary means:
1. Study of truths underlying being and knowledge.
2. System of philosophical belief.
3. Principles of particular field of knowledge or action.

It can also be said that the ultimate nature of reality is the unknown or the higher truths.

The study of the Electromagnetic Body is a science of matter, motion, energy, force and a change, as in metamorphosis. The word, metamorphosis, is a very apt term because a person who is not well, undergoes a tremendous metamorphosis to well-being as their Base Electromagnetic Body is repaired and restored. Hence, based on these definitions, Metaphysician is an aptly coined title.

In Metaphysics, we are utilizing a branch of philosophy concerned with the ultimate nature of reality. The ultimate nature of reality, is that there is much that exists that is not visible to the naked eye without clairvoyant sight. Therefore, Metaphysicians are doctors of the invisible Spiritual Bodies, which encompass, The Electromagnetic Body, The Mental Body, and The Emotional Body and the Sub-Systems, which we will go into more in Chapter 4. Metaphysics exactly describes the nature of the Electromagnetic Body and Energy Medicine because *both are invisible yet are the ultimate nature of reality.*

Because the Spiritual Bodies are invisible to the naked eye, they are not easily comprehended or understood by the majority of the world. This is very sad because so many people could thrive instead of just survive, living with poor health, which generates a lack of joy and enthusiasm for life. My hope is that through this book there will be a much greater understanding of how true healing occurs on a natural basis through the Spiritual Bodies and Energy Medicine, without drugs, needles or surgery.

A simple explanation of how a miraculous healing takes place is this; repairs are made to the various Spiritual Bodies through the Electromagnetic Body, The Emotional Body, The Mental Body and the many Sub-Systems that exist, which then allows the physical body to heal itself naturally without pain, pills, needles or surgery. Is there anyone who would not want to restore good health without being on needless drugs, without pain, without needles and/or surgery? God gave us everything we need for the body to heal itself given the right tools.

For a miraculous healing to take place, the Energy Medicine Practitioner must have a good understanding of the Electromagnetic Body in order to determine which repair is necessary. To give you an example of another sort, suppose your car will not start. Does the mechanic repair the engine instead of suspecting that the car will not start because of the battery or the ignition? No, the mechanic checks the battery and the ignition before he moves on to the engine. The same theory is applicable to the Electromagnetic Body; the proper technique and frequency or vibration must be utilized. Once the repair is made to the Electromagnetic Body, a secondary result occurs, as the physical body can now heal itself on a natural basis.

To get to a level where an Energy Practitioner can perform these miraculous healings, they must learn in-depth practical, mechanical and spiritual application of how the various Spiritual Bodies affects the Physical Body. However, more importantly, they have to undergo much healing themselves in order to raise their own vibration. They have to raise their vibration or frequency sufficiently high enough to reach certain frequencies or vibrations in order to perform these techniques successfully. This is because Energy Medicine operates by variations of frequency, sound and vibration. Additionally, different techniques may require a variety of unique hands-on technique, plus frequencies, sounds and/or vibrations to heal a particular disorder.

In order for Energy Medicine to work, an Energy Medicine Practitioner is required to have a much higher or greater vibration than most people's frequency or vibration. To give you an example, many people are the color green in an Aura Photograph, which has a frequency of 250-475 hertz, whereas a healer is most likely dark blue, dark pink or magenta. These colors have a frequency anywhere from 1,500 to 2,800 mega hertz. This information is part of the research that was done in developing Aura Technology. *(As an aside, one of the known Names of God is Magenta, which is a very dark pink, almost purple, color).*

All illness has a particular frequency or vibration, and there is a particular vibration or frequency that is necessary to heal that illness. This is why the doctor gives you a pill. The doctor is attempting to reach the necessary vibration or frequency that will heal that particular ailment through the pill. So following this thought, if a particular repair is needed and the energy practitioner cannot reach the vibration or frequency needed to perform the necessary repairs, the repair will obviously not be made. This is why some energy practitioners have great success and others have little success. The practitioner also needs a good understanding of the Physical Body in order to relate the symptoms to what techniques to use so that healing will occur through the Electromagnetic Body.

My area of expertise is in how to repair the Electromagnetic Body, which as a secondary result, allows the Physical Body to heal itself. This is because it is the Electromagnetic Body that feeds the Physical Body the energy for life itself, and it supersedes the Physical Body. Hence, if the Electromagnetic Body is damaged or sick, then so are we on a physical basis.

Energy practitioners have the ability to sense, feel or see where a blockage lies. This is necessary in order to find out what the challenge is, and then perform the necessary techniques to repair the ailment. It is important to understand that not all Energy Practitioners are of the same caliber. Some have a rudimentary knowledge of the Electromagnetic Body, and some have an expanded knowledge. You might liken this to the family doctor, who will often refer you to a specialist, because he cannot perform surgery or cure cancer but he can assist you with the common cold, flu or ear infection.

Energy practitioners with higher insights and gifts are using the very same "Gifts Of The Spirit" referenced in the Bible. There are nine gifts of the Spirit listed in the Bible. These gifts are given by God to those he chooses to use to assist humanity. The nine gifts listed below are from the New American Standard Bible, as follows:

1 Corinthians 12:4-1. Now there are a varieties of gifts, but the same Spirit. 5. And there are varieties of ministries and the same Lord. 6. And there are varieties of effect, but the same God who works all things in all persons. 7. But to each one is given the manifestation of the Spirit for the common good. 8. For to one is given the word of wisdom through the Spirit, and to another the word of knowledge according to the same Spirit; 9. to another faith by the same Spirit, and to another gifts of healing by the one Spirit, 10 and to another the effecting of miracles, and to another prophecy, and to another the distinguishing of spirits, to another various kinds of tongues and to another the interpretation of tongues. 11. But one and the same Spirit works all of these things, distributing to each one individually just as He wills.

1. Wisdom
2. Knowledge
3. Faith
4. Healing
5. Effecting miracles
6. Prophecy
7. Distinguishing of spirits
8. Hearing in various tongues (languages)
9. Speaking in various tongues (languages)

Most of us have faith in God, who is unseen, unknown and mysterious. A large majority of us believe in angels, who are also invisible. Most of us believe in ghosts, which, again, are invisible. The very word *faith* indicates *belief without sight*. What I am attempting to show you and want you to understand that there is much more to the universe than what we can see with the naked eye. This includes the Electromagnetic Body.

It has been my experience that the majority of people can be taught to tune into their higher senses with a little help. When I give a lecture, I usually execute an interactive group participation exercise whereby everyone learns to sense, feel or see the Electromagnetic Body. Somewhere between eighty-five to ninety-five percent of the group can feel or sense the Electromagnetic Body the first time they try to in a guided attempt.

I have had a lot of fun with skeptical participants who have taken part in this exercise to rule out the possibility of being able to feel or sense the Electromagnetic Body or Aura. Boy, were they surprised to find out they were completely wrong. Recently, one woman who said she was a *skeptic,* took part in the exercise and became totally freaked out upon finding out she could feel and sense the Aura. She exclaimed over and over again, *Oh My God, Oh My God, Oh My God.* In fact, she was so freaked out that she had to take a few minutes to compose herself before she could finish the exercise. I call this a *spontaneous awakening.*

The word, Aura, is sometimes used interchangeably in place of the title, The Electromagnetic Body. This is because it is a simplified explanation of the Electromagnetic Body and the Electromagnetic Body is contained within its field. Many people have heard of the Aura, maybe, even read a book about it, learning about the colors of the Aura and the chakras. The chakras are an intricate component of the Electromagnetic Body. Most people have heard of the Aura, which surrounds your body that is filled with swirling colors and energy. It is shaped like a big egg or balloon. When I interpret an Aura Photograph of the seven chakras, I read the aura photo the way a doctor would read an x-ray. An Aura Photograph can tell you a great deal about a person's health and well-being. Additionally, I believe that an Aura Photograph is the closest thing that you will ever come to seeing your Soul. Should you have the opportunity to get an Aura Photograph, I would highly encourage you to get it done. If there is a printout available, I would be certain to get the report, as it will tell you where you are in your journey on this Earth on a spiritual, mental and emotional basis. Aura Photography is generally available at most Mind, Body and Spirit Expos.

Another challenge that exists is that, as a general rule, people do not like change. Most people brought up in the United States know only one form of medicine, traditional medicine. Our health care system is probably one of the best in the world, but it generally works by treating a symptom. Very rarely, does it get to the root of the problem and resolve the root problem.

Let us take an example of high cholesterol. High cholesterol is a result of the body being too acidic. The acidic challenge occurs because the person is eating too many acidic foods, such as meat and sugar, especially in the form of cereals, pretzels, pasta, bread, cookies, cakes, etc. All of these simple carbohydrates convert to sugar. The liver is doing its job by rushing cholesterol to a blood vessel, where the blood has become so acidic that it wants to burn a hole right through the vessel, causing hemorrhage and possible death. Cholesterol is rushed to the scene of crisis, laying down cholesterol and calcium to cover the area where there is a weakening in the blood vessel, and possible hemorrhage so that the person does not bleed to death.

What does the doctor tell you to do? Take this pill to lower your cholesterol. If the plaque is removed totally and your blood is still too acidic and no cholesterol is rushed to the scene, what do you think might happen? The answer is that there is the potential for the blood vessel to hemorrhage. In my opinion, a better way to go that gets to the root of the problem would be to advise them to change their diet to alkaline foods, along with taking cholesterol vitamins, since the cholesterol drugs are know to cause many side effects. An alkaline diet is one that is primarily a plant-based diet filled with a lot of vegetables and fruits. This eliminates simple carbohydrates and too much meat. You will quickly see how your cholesterol levels will fall. You may need to take cholesterol medicine or cholesterol vitamins until the levels have a chance to come down though since by diet alone may take a month or more.

To give you an example, my husbands' cholesterol was too high so he stopped eating bread, pasta and his beloved Tasty cakes by about fifty percent. Within a month his cholesterol dropped sixty points. This is a clear example of what food choices will do for you.

He decided to stop eating as much bread and pasta because of the book (Eat Right For Your Blood Type) by Dr. D'Amato. Dr. D'Amato performed many clinical trials and believes that different foods, work for different blood types. He believes that wheat, is a food intolerance for a person with type 0 blood type. In addition, influencing his decision was Dr. Simon, who is an excellent holistic Chiropractic Doctor, and is a big proponent of not eating simple carbohydrates.

However, this is not seeing the whole picture because cholesterol means on a spiritual level, *that you are squeezing the joy out of life.* This could be because you are under stress, perhaps you are a workaholic and do not take time to play, only work, work, work. Alternatively, perhaps there are financial reasons, and/or any number of reasons. The point I am making is that unless you address the spiritual cause, even shifting to a plant based diet will not lower the cholesterol permanently, because you have not shifted the spiritual reason behind it.

Another challenge is that Energy Medicine is not covered by medical insurance. The majority of Americans who have health coverage want to maximize the medical coverage instead of paying out of their pocket for natural health care. However, by utilizing Alternative and Complementary Medicine, such as Energy Medicine, Chiropractic Care and Massage, combined with a plant-based diet and exercise, we would be so healthy that we would not get sick. We would thrive instead of simply survive.

CHAPTER 3 ~

How Does The Electromagnetic Body Get Damaged?

Let me explain what has happened to damage the Electromagnetic Body, hence the Physical Body. Everything that exists has a frequency or energy to it, especially electronic devices such as computers, TVs, telephones, faxes, cell phones, refrigerators, microwaves, alarm clocks that sit right next to our heads at night, electric blankets that we lay over our bodies, and wireless technology.

As a Professional Aura Photographer, on many occasions, I have seen holes in the Electromagnetic Body on the right or left side of the lower Electromagnetic Body that immediately signal to me that they are sitting with their leg next to a computer tower frequently. I also see many other holes in common places such as around the ears, colon or liver areas, as a result of having a cell phone or other electrical device on their belt or ear. I often find holes in the Electromagnetic Body right around the center torso, immediately indicating that this person is probably using a laptop frequently. It has been my personal experience that each and every time I have had a dental x-ray, mammogram, CAT scan, MRI or bone scan that I have had to repair holes in my Electromagnetic Body. Therefore, the sick get sicker, as their energy and life force slips out through these holes in their Electromagnetic Body.

Other ways we damage our Electromagnetic Body are simple accidents. How many of us, as we were learning to walk, fell down? All of us fell down at one time or another! How many of us played sports, roller-skated, ice skated, played football or baseball? Did any of us fall down when we did this? Of course we did. Did any of us climb trees when we were younger? Did we fall down? Of course we did. How many of us have had broken bones? Many of us have. How many of us have been having dental work since we were a small child? Can you count how many times you have had x-rays? One of the reasons the sick get sicker is the sheer volume of tests to which we are subjected to that damage the Electromagnetic Body.

How many car accidents have you had? How many fights did you get into as a youngster? Did you ever crack your head? All of these things create damage that is sight unseen, which eventually filters down to our Physical Body.

Additionally, let me give another way that our Electromagnetic Body gets damaged. Visualize that we are walking through a dust storm that is electromagnetic in nature and this dust gets absorbed by us. The Electromagnetic Body absorbs electromagnetic frequencies from birth. Also, as we simply walk through life, our Electromagnetic Body is absorbing other peoples' negative energies. Every lifetime that you have had, you have absorbed these energies, which carry through to the next life if not removed.

Add to this any emotional or mental traumas, which carry enteric wounds or scars from lifetime to lifetime, until these scars are removed and repairs are made. The majority of these electromagnetic energies are of a lower vibration or frequency. As the energy is absorbed by your Electromagnetic Body or Aura, it goes through your prana tube to your charkas, to your meridians, to your nerves, to your organs, and to your very cells, clogging all of these esoteric or physical organs. As your body becomes clogged with these lower vibrations or frequencies, the law of *like attracts like* occurs, thus attracting more negative energies to you. It is a vicious cycle. After an Energy Medicine Healing has taken place, you are now clear to attract higher more positive vibrations to yourself. This enables you to feel more peaceful and joyful, to be more balanced as the negative energies are now gone from your being.

Another way to think of how your Electromagnetic Body gets damaged is to think of driving your car for 200,000 miles and never changing the oil. Think of how gummed up the oil filter would be, as well as the car's engine, transmission, spark plugs and every other mechanical part. This is similar to how your body gets gummed up with negative energies. Once you are purged and cleared of these negative frequencies or vibrations, you might compare it to having changed the oil and filter in your car every 3,000 miles so that the car can operate efficiently and properly. After an Energy Medicine clearing and healing session, the body can operate efficiently, properly and thus have the ability to heal itself.

I am personally convinced that chronic fatigue, lymphoma, fluid around the heart, some heart challenges, liver problems and an inestimable host of other illnesses are a result of the entire body being gummed up with these negative energies. Once your body is purged, your Electromagnetic Body can heal itself with the right techniques. After you have all of the negative energies removed, a secondary result will be more happiness, peace and joy in your life from the universal law of *like attracts like.*

Another thing that damages your Electromagnetic Body are negative thought processes. Let me explain how this happens. Everything starts on a spiritual level. This is because, in the spiritual realm and other dimensions, everyone can communicate by telepathy. There is really no need for words. However, just as it states in the Bible, that God created the world by his *Words.* When we *speak negative words,* such as *I am so tired* or *I am so sick,* you will be tired and you will be sick because you are creating this by your *own words.*

You must speak to the solution and not the problem. To give you an example, if you are sick, the way to get well is to say, *I am very well, I am getting better every day, or I am fantastic*, instead of continuing to create your own sickness. Because your mind is like a computerized robot, if it hears, *I am sick* or *I am tired*, this is what it will create in your body. This is the *mental level*. When you add feelings into the mix, such as saying these words in the fullness with feelings of sadness, tiredness and lack of enthusiasm, *I am so….tired*, you throw a log onto the smothering coals, which now creates a flame. You see, your *words* have more power than you can imagine. God created the world through His *Word* and we all have a spark of our Creator in us. So you can see how this process works. This is the *emotional level*. Through these processes, of the Electromagnetic Body, the Mental Body, and the Emotional Body, illness can easily be created. In this given scenario, the frequency levels of these negative thought processes are extremely low.

People who have a negative outlook not only attract negative vibrations to them, but also negative people, as people that appear in your life are nothing more than a mirror of yourself.

There has been a big flurry in recent years of books that address this very subject from (*The Secret*) to (*The Moses Code*), all dealing with how we are *co-creators* of our very own reality. We are not *victims* because we create these circumstances ourselves. However, we are not very wise to do so and now you will know better. It takes a significant amount of self-discipline to change your negative thought processes, but you can do it. When you say something negative, such as *I feel so sick today,* you can turn it around by saying, *but I am feeling better moment by moment.* Or, *I am so tired,* you can add to your statement of woe by saying, *but I am feeling more energetic by the second.*

Do you see how simple this is? The theory might be simple, but it is not easy to change the entire way you speak or present yourself. It might take anywhere from six months to several years to change negative thinking, which I call *stinking thinking.* Learn to talk to yourself in a healthy, wealthy and wise way. Learn to say instead, *I am getting wiser by the day, I am getting healthier by the day.* Do you see what I mean?

In the Chapter 7, there is a section called, *The Manual,* that will give you the spiritual reason behind physical afflictions. This is important, because you must address the spiritual cause before you can heal on a permanent basis. Otherwise, an illness will just keep coming back over and over again.

CHAPTER 4 ~

Four Main Bodies And Their Sub-Systems.

The cure for the part should not be attempted without treatment of the whole.

Plato

There are four main bodies and many entire sub-systems that need to be healed in order to be whole. These different sub-systems are encompassed in The Spiritual Body. These four main bodies are The Electromagnetic Body, The Emotional Body, The Mental Body, and The Physical Body. There are many sub-systems that exist in these various four bodies, which are listed below:

THE SUB-SYSTEMS:

- The Meridian System
- The Grid System,
- The Chakra System,
- The Prana Tube
- The Psychic System
- The Blueprint System & The Assemblage Point
- Acu-Flow points,
- Chi-points or gateways
- The Batteries
- The Reserves
- The Crystal System

THE ELECTROMAGNETIC BODY

The Electromagnetic Body plays a huge part in our health because it is the Electromagnetic Body that feeds us the energy for our very life itself. Cut off the energy, cut off the life. If you think about the fact that when a death occurs, all of the body parts are intact, the blood system is intact, and the nervous and lymph systems are intact. So what is missing that death occurred? Energy! Energy! Energy is the right answer! Encompassed in the Electromagnetic Body are many total individual systems, which are listed in the above paragraph.

All of these systems work together to send your Physical Body the energy necessary for you to exist. If there are breaks, blockages, or tears in any of these systems, you can be sure that your Physical Body will soon start to suffer the consequences. I am convinced that most, if not all illness, mental or physical, is the result of some malfunction of our Spirit, which as a consequence of this malfunction or miscreation, affects the other bodies. Working with Energy Medicine and these Spiritual Bodies, I have seen complete miraculous resolution of even chronic diseases, such as ADHD, Asthma, Diabetes, Heart Challenges, Edema, Fibromyalgia, Chronic Fatigue Syndrome, Herniated Discs, Mental Illness, Epilepsy, Depression, Hypertension, Edema, and Chronic Pulmonary Disease. Almost all manner of sickness or illness can be helped by the healing of The Spiritual Body, through the Electromagnetic Body and Energy Medicine. It is simply miraculous to witness these chronic conditions do a complete turn around.

There are many different modalities that are practiced worldwide, such as Reiki, (which at last count has about eight million practitioners), Pranic Healing, Healing Touch, Frequency Balancing, Emotional Freedom Technique (EFT), Whole Life Healing, Tapas Acupuncture Technique (TAT), Be Set Free Fast, Integrated Energy Therapy (IET), Jin Shin Jyutsu, Quantum Touch, Holographic Repatterning, 24 Strand DNA Activation, and The Reconnection.

There are many more modalities that exist that heal on a natural basis. There are so many modalities that I am sure I don't know all of them.

There are thousands of practitioners of Feng Shui, which is a much larger form of energy work, working with property and the land. Heck, even Donald Trump uses Feng Shui when he decorates his casinos. I read this in the local newspaper. Then there are the Buddhist Monks from Tibet, Chinese Practitioners and Doctors, Hindu Practitioners and Doctors, all of whom work with the Mind, Body and Spirit. In the eastern medical community, there is much more of an emphasis placed on the whole system of Body, Mind and Spirit in an attempt to get to the root of the problem rather than treating just the symptoms.

In China, if a person is diagnosed with Cancer, instead of being given radiation, chemotherapy and surgery, he might be given a prescription to practice Qigong or Tai Chi for six months, take a particular herb, and come back in a few months. Have you seen on television groups of people in China practicing a morning ritual of Tai Chi and Qigong? This is a common practice in public, where all join in these exercises in their common areas and parks.

These practices that involve The Body, Mind and Spirit are one of the reasons the Chinese are known to have an extremely long and healthy life, despite being about ten years behind the western world in traditional medical practices and surgery. It is also very rare to see an obese Chinese person because they eat an alkaline plant-based diet, with animal protein more as a condiment to the meal than the main course, thereby bypassing conditions such as high cholesterol. They do not even have a word for menopause because their women do not experience the same level of decline that American women experience. This is due to eating a diet consistently filled with plant-based estrogens and Chinese herbs that balance the body. These herbs that balance the body are typically called adaptogens.

If you have heard of Acupuncture, you may have heard of the meridians. Acupuncture works by sticking needles into Acu-flow points to break up energetic blocks and stimulate energy flow. The meridians are a circulatory system through which energy flows to feed the organs, nerves and cells. You might think of the meridians as the hoses and wires in a car that connect all of the various components. If your radiator hose blows, your car will overheat and will not run without the radiator circulating the fluid through the car. The same is true of our circulatory meridian system.

There are different layers of grids weaving all of the bodies together, which connect to the meridians. Everyone should have at least seven strong grid layers, working in harmony with the Chakra System. You might think of the Grid System as the chassis on a car. If you get a minor dent or hole in your car, the car will usually still run, as will the body. But if you sustain a major dent, such as smashing in the front of your car, the car will not be able to run. The same thing occurs with our bodies. Eventually the body will not be able to run and will develop some fatigue syndrome or possibly heart challenges. This is because the heart has to work extra hard trying to keep the energy flowing throughout the body. If it has major holes leaking energy out of the Electromagnetic Body's Grid System, the heart is overworked until it just cannot run anymore.

The Chakra System has seven primary chakras, routinely discussed in many books, and has hundreds of secondary chakras. Illness will generally manifest in the area of a blocked chakra.

For instance, if your Sacral Chakra is blocked, you may have female problems or fertility problems. Men may have prostate problems and your sex life may tank. You may have problems with your lower back, your stomach or your legs.

Another analogy is to think of the chakras as the sparkplugs of a car. If one of the sparkplugs or chakras is clogged or blocked, the entire car does not run right; nor will your body. The seven chakras that are well known are the:

• Root Chakra	~	Bottom of your torso
• Sacral Chakra	~	Below your belly button
• Solar Plexus Chakra	~	Above your belly button
• Heart Chakra	~	Center of your chest
• Throat Chakra	~	Throat area
• Third Eye Chakra	~	Forehead
• Crown Chakra	~	Top of your head

The Prana Tube is the primary central component through which energy is stored and circulated. You might think of it as the gas tank in a vehicle. It is the main storage area for our life force. It looks like a long tube that runs from above your head to below your feet. The seven main chakras sit within this central tube. The chakras absorb the energy from the Prana Tube, and send it to the meridians. The energy is then diverted through the meridians and Grid System to the nervous system, organs and cellular structure.

The Assemblage Point is a circle that is centered in the middle of the chest and a main part of your Blueprint System. When your Blueprint is perfect balance, you will find the Assemblage Point in the center of your chest. When the Blueprint is not in perfect balance, the Assemblage Point is splintered into many different parts all over your body. When someone is in perfect harmony, perfect balance, wonderfully healthy on all levels of being, mental, emotional, psychic, spiritual, and electromagnetic, there will exist this one main point in the center of the chest. This will fall naturally into place as the body is healed. Since so few people are in perfect harmony and balance, the assemblage point usually has splintered into many areas of the body.

There are some practitioners who try to move the assemblage points back to where they belong in the center of the chest. However, I have found that until a person has experienced total balancing amongst all the bodies, that the assemblage point will splinter and bounce right back to where they were before. Usually, you will find them all over the Electromagnetic Body. If you find that someone has one main assemblage point, you know that you are dealing with a healthy, balanced, and most likely, evolved individual.

Acu-Flow points are little tiny pools of energy that act as a bridge or a stop gate, depending on what is needed at the time. They are found running up and down all of the primary meridians in the body. If a person develops a break in a meridian, the Acu-Flow point will act as a stop gate. What this does is prevent energy from spewing out into unprotected areas of the body. To give you an example, if you were to plug in an extension cord and then cut it with a pair of scissors, the energy would spew out chaotically and probably electrocute you. This is the same thing that occurs when a meridian has a break in it. Chaotic energy spews into the body, causing a great deal of damage if not for the Acu-Flow points. Even with the help of the stop gates or Acu-Flow points, there will still be some chaotic energy that will most probably disrupt the energy of the body. There are thousands, if not millions, of Acu-Flow points in the body.

Chi-points are access points that enable energy practitioners to access the front and the back of the body at the same time. For instance, if a person is lying on their back, you can access the back of the body through the front gateways, or Chi-points. Naturally, if someone is lying on their stomach, you can access the front of the body through the back gateways or Chi-points. The Battery System is a back-up system of energy reserved to run your body when the organs have used up their energy which when replenished, renews your energy, zest and joy.

The Reserve System is similar to your Battery System except that it is an energy reserve for your Mental and Emotional Bodies. As this system runs low on energy, this is one of the reasons that as we age, we lose our mental flexibility and emotional agility.

The Crystal System is a complete system unto itself that assists in running the Electromagnetic Body and amplifies our energy when repaired and turned on fully.

The Mental Body

On the other side, the other dimensions, or the Heavenlies, however you want to say it, there is no reason to vocalize, as everyone is telepathic. This is also how prophets or psychics hear, through telepathy. When the Bible talks about the *Word,* we get the picture that the *Word* is a very important thing, since God created the world by His *Word.* When words are spoken aloud, it is a stronger measure of a thought process. Yet, when you think in your mind negative, bad or evil thoughts, Spirit picks it up as though it were *words.* To change your life, *you need to change not only your words but also your very thoughts.* It has been my experience that thoughts enter your mind unbidden and we must constantly be on the alert for negative thoughts, as they can be our undoing. If you have a negative thought such as "I am so fat," you can catch yourself and add, "But I am getting thinner every day." Let me give you some examples:

- "I am so dumb," "but I am getting smarter by the moment"
- "I am so tired," "but I am more energized by the minute"
- "I am so sick," "but I am getting better and better each day"
- "I am so lonely," "but I am going to meet new friends very soon"
- "I hate my job," "and I am going to find a new job that is perfect for me"
- "I hate this dress;" "I'm going shopping for a new dress I will love"
- "I am so broke," "but I am manifesting more money by the moment"
- Do you get the picture? This is what you must do because whatever we think is attracted to us like a magnet. Like attracts like. At this moment in time, I understand that there is only a five-minute gap between when we think something and when it will automatically manifest for those who have reached this evolved stage.

The Emotional Body

The Emotional Body is very important because it is either the fuel that makes us healthy, wealthy and wise, or the fuel that creates poor health, poor finances and unwise thoughts. Let me explain. When a person is crying, they are obviously very sad or upset on an emotional basis. When a person gets angry, they may say unkind things, slam doors, break things and make everyone else miserable. When a person is worried about a lack of money, this emotion creates just what they don't want, a lack of money. Soon, unexpected bills arrive in the mail and create a loss of more money. Buried anger is behind a lot of depressed people. It is anger turned inward. Fear, however, is the biggest of all emotions. Fear keeps us living in the dark, depressed and unhappy. Fear is behind almost all emotions except love, hope, compassion and forgiveness. You must remember to turn away from fear and look to the positive instead.

Most people live their lives in subconscious fear, fearing to move forward because they may make a mistake, fearing to leave the job they hate because they may not get another job, etc. Overweight people typically have more fear issues than thin people, since the excess weight is a form of protection. Most of the time, these emotions are on a sub-conscious basis and we are unaware that we are living in sub-conscious fear. A good anagram for FEAR is, *false evidence appearing real.*

My motto has always been to dive right into what we desire and fear be damned. I have always lived my life this way and have found that it works for me. I have developed an Energy Medicine Technique that I call, *Healing the Inner Child,* which resolves these emotional issues, and is a thousand times more potent than any other resource or tool I know of. However, it must be used cautiously because of it potency and can only be used every three or four months. It may take a year or more to resolve our *Inner Child,* on a case-by-case basis. However, what are all of these emotions trying to do? They are trying to get you to pay attention to your emotions, to understand why you are depressed, angry, fearful, or sad, so that you can overcome these emotional blocks.

You must RULE FEAR, not let fear rule you. A courageous man or woman goes forward, despite fear. This is why it is called, *courage. You have fear, but you don't let it control or cripple you.* In other words, emotions are the fuel that expounds what we want or do not want, based on our thought processes. Fear does not cripple a courageous person. It motivates them to overcome the fear, to go forward and make use of the courage that God gave us all. Order up a large portion of courage and use it by saying, *I have all of the courage I need to overcome all of my fears. I move forward despite fear. I RULE FEAR.*

The Physical Body

The Physical Body is obviously the one that is most understood because we can see it, feel it, sense it, hear it, and taste it. In fact, most people believe that the Physical Body is really all that there is to our existence. Obviously, the challenge lies in the fact that, for the most part, there is no physical proof that the unseen realms exist, but I guarantee you, they most certainly do. A good example of unseen things that exist is the oxygen that we need to breathe. We cannot see it but it is there nonetheless. Some people even believe that there is no God and no afterlife. I would like you to entertain the idea that there might be far more than the physical realm, more than you can possibly imagine. Most people take it on faith that there is more, and believe that we live on in Heaven after we die.

I do not dismiss that the physical body has needs that should be supported while undergoing the transition from being ill to being well. If medication is necessary, take it while you get well. If there are no other options except surgery, get the surgery. However, for most people, if their Electromagnetic Body is repaired and maintained, they will be in just about perfect health. Of course, being in perfect health requires a good attitude, good food and exercise too, in addition to having the Electromagnetic Body repaired. It is when we let things go on for too long that we must resort to medication or surgery.

I will give you an example. One of my associates, Joann, had a problem with her ovaries. Her hair was starting to thin out on top. She had excessive hair on her face for a woman. She had severe pain in her abdomen, around the ovaries, from ovarian cysts. This problem had been going on for some time. Because Joann was a Karma Master, she thought she should run karma sessions and that was the only way to restore her health. I could not agree more; except that I would have considered the fact that, she most probably had a hormonal imbalance that could have been corrected with bio-identical hormones. This is a clear case of needing medicine to support the body while she was working through her karma. Additionally, I would have considered the spiritual cause behind the challenge with the ovaries. The spiritual cause behind problems with the ovaries is, *fear of the sexual role, also being lonely with a lack of love.* See in Chapter 7, The Manual under the subtitle, ovaries, for what can be done to resolve this particular challenge. Even in a committed relationship, there can be loneliness by feeling a disconnection from a loved one. The reason I stress this is that, without acknowledging the spiritual cause behind the physical problem, the physical cannot be permanently healed. The challenge will just keep reoccurring until the spiritual cause is resolved.

This is one of the reasons that cancer continues to reoccur repeatedly, because the spiritual reason behind it was never addressed. No one receives counseling to address an underlying spiritual cause when cancer rears its ugly head in the western world of medicine. You can fix the physical all you want to, but unless you address the spiritual cause, it will simply reoccur. There are thousands, perhaps millions, of books written about the Physical Body, so I will stop here since this book is about healing the Physical Body through the invisible bodies of the Electromagnetic Body.

The Psychic Body-(A Sub-System)

The Psychic Body has many ethereal components of which you may or may not be aware of. You have a psychic center, which is centered on your lower face and upper chest area. The Psychic Body is responsible for being able to see with the inner eye what you cannot see with the outer eyes and to hear with the inner ear what you cannot hear with the outer ears. This is what is meant in the Bible when Jesus said, *Those who have ears to hear, let them hear.* This is Spirit talking to you. Many times, when I give a lecture, I do an interactive exercise, which demonstrates, to everyone that most people can learn to see, feel or sense the Aura. During the interactive exercise, people report feeling different sensations, such as pressure in their chest, tingling in their hands or their body, and pressure in their forehead or around their ears. They sometimes feel heat in their hands or body, or they might feel cold or tingling.

Other people report a feeling in their stomach or a knowing. Everyone is different, experiencing different sensations and feelings that are very subtle. Yet, we can be trained to recognize them for what they are, signals given to us that are of a psychic nature. Most of us, at one time or another, knew who was on the phone when the phone rang, or had a bad feeling in our gut when we suddenly sensed something was wrong. These feelings and sensations are all a part of the Psychic Body.

Does anyone remember that television show, (My Favorite Martian)? Well, antennas such as the ones he had do exist in our etheric body. We have many antennas that crisscross our bodies and run through our chakras. God gives these ideas to TV directors and writers so that people can understand these concepts in a comfortable way. If suddenly you were given psychic sight and could see the Electromagnetic Body, you might be scared to death, if you didn't have any idea of what you were observing. You might think that the person you were observing had suddenly morphed into a giant ant or a scary monster.

Everyone has these antennas that pick up telepathic thoughts, similar to radio waves. One of the reasons not everyone is a prophet or psychic, is because the antennas have a tendency to get pushed downward during the birthing process, and do not automatically spring back up. Some of the most prophetic people I know have had a breech birth, which means that the antennas are pushed upright that can catch the telepathic signals. Do you remember the TV antennas that we used to call rabbit ears, and how you had to jiggle them around to get them in just the right position in order to receive a good picture on the TV? The antennas we possess are very similar. I have good news for those of you who have always wanted to be clairvoyant or psychic; all is not yet lost. These psychic body parts can be straightened and repaired so that you too can receive telepathic signals.

Another reason everyone is not psychic is because of damage to the antennas from falls, accidents, etc. Other body parts that are responsible for psychic ability are the pineal and pituitary glands. These glands are part of the endocrine system. When we were children, many of us had invisible friends, but as our parents told us not to talk about our invisible friends, we lost the ability to see, hear or talk to them.

As a child, our third eye is open, but as we age, if we do not use these psychic abilities, we lose them as a calcium shield grows over the third eye. Also, it is not very difficult to sustain damage to these delicate organs from cracking your head in a fall or car accident. I know a few people who had sustained only whiplash during an accident and yet lost their psychic abilities, most likely because the pituitary and/or pineal glands sustained some damage. These are very fragile organs and are easily damaged.

Spiritual Body

The definition for *Spirit* in Webster's Dictionary is:

1. A vital principle in humanity; soul.
2. Supernatural being.

I find that both of these definitions are exactly right. The Spiritual Body is a supernatural being, and guess who that supernatural being is? You are! The Spiritual Body is your very Soul that is encompassed in your Electromagnetic Body, with all of the other components, the Mental, the Emotional, the Physical and the Psychic Bodies. This is who we truly are, a spirit having an earthly experience, not a human having a spiritual experience. Only a very small part of our Soul exists in our bodies. The larger part of our Soul is called, *our Higher Self and/or our Over Soul* by many who are spiritually enlightened. The Higher Self and/or Over Soul is known to exist in the ninth chakra, which sits two chakras above your crown chakra, which is in the center of the top of your head.

If you would like to learn more about the chakras, I suggest you go to your local bookstore and pick up a book on it. There are thousands of books that have been written exclusively about these spinning wheels of energy that feed our bodies. I will go more into the chakra system in Chapter 5. However, it would take an entire book written *only on* chakras to receive the entire picture. The larger part of our Soul stays in Spirit, overseeing all that we are supposed to be learning here in this school called Earth, where we came to grow our Souls and fulfill our mission. Many times people feel that they are victimized by bad circumstances. However, I believe that bad circumstances are one of three things, listed below:

The first is that you, in the physical, are creating what is happening to you by your very thoughts and words.

- The second is that your Higher-Self or Over-Soul may be redirecting you, if you are not on your path fulfilling what you came here to do. Believe me, your Soul will cause you to have lessons, so that you do what you came here to do.

- Third, you may be paying off some of your karma. With any of these reasons, these harsh circumstances are a self-creation from you, either in the physical, or from your own Soul in the spiritual.

CHAPTER 5 ~

Repairing and Building To A New Body

Are you ready to learn the secrets of YATUVAY and how many miraculous healings are able to occur? Are you ready to communicate with God on a one-on-one basis?. Are you ready to experience the most profound feeling that you have ever experienced from working directly with The Father? If so, continue to read on because you are about to learn how to experience, *The Power of One! The Power of One is the Power of God!* It is God who determines if the "Power of One" will be shared and with whom. I can make no promises in this regard, but I do know that those who are pure of heart and have been called into service by God, will be granted the "Power of One" if your system can handle the power of it. If your system is not up to task yet, the energy will revert to the Ascension Healing Energy under the umbrella of my work, where you will still work with God but will not have the "Power of One". This is the very best quality of healing energy you will find other than YATUVAY, which grants the *Power of one.*

I will teach you a synopsis of all but one of the Basic-Seven-Step-Repair-System that lay the groundwork for the more advanced techniques in the YATUVAY Coursework. This way you can get started right away with resolving many of the challenges that you, your loved ones and/or your clients face. The Basic-Seven-Step-Repair-System, will resolve seventy to eighty-five percent of the challenges that you will run into. However, some of the remaining, more advanced techniques mentioned in Chapter 7, The Manual, are a *unique hands-on technique* that must be learned in its fullness, in a classroom setting with in-depth knowledge. Additionally, some of the techniques are extremely advanced and cannot be fully explained in this book, as it takes almost a book to understand each individual technique. However, those of you who are a Master of Energy Medicine will already understand these techniques and know what it will take to complete the healing process. If not, you can always sign up for the necessary coursework.

In Chapter 4, I talked about the different components that make up the Spiritual Body through the

Electromagnetic Body. In Chapter 5, I am going to explain the mechanics of repairing the Electromagnetic Body in more detail. Are you ready to get started?

The very first thing *that must be done* is to clear the body of any negative energy. Otherwise, by a co-mingling of energy from the healer and the client, the healer's body will become polluted with the negative energy from the patient's body. Remember that I mentioned previously that a healer's energy system needs a much higher frequency than other people, in order to be an effective healer? This is so that they can reach the height of the frequency necessary to utilize a specific technique. If a healer becomes polluted from the client's negative energy, and they do not know how to, or do not religiously cleanse themselves, they will not be able to maintain the height of a frequency for very long. This carries with it a serious repercussion of making them sick too.

A person with a lot of negative energy will most likely be anxious, fearful, sad, and angry, since negative energy is a much lower vibration. Once this negative energy is removed, a person will feel much happier, more peaceful, and will experience better health. There is a doctor who has done some marvelous work in what I call, Energetic Hygiene, by the name of Dr. Modi, MD. Dr. Modi is a psychiatrist who discovered that about eighty percent of her patients' experienced immediate wellness after the patients' negative energy was successfully removed. Her results are a validation to me of my own work. Dr. Modi, M.D. wrote a book called, (Remarkable Healings-A Psychiatrist Discovers Unsuspected Roots of Mental and Physical Illness) in which this information was shared.

Everyone has the potential to have healing abilities. It was been placed in your Blueprint when you were created. It is a question of having your healing abilities activated, raising your own vibrations sufficiently high enough, and learning the required knowledge on a mechanical and spiritual basis. Some of you will already be activated from previous Energy Medicine Classes or from prior energetic work done. Others will not be and will need to be energetically activated.

However, before we can embark on a healing session, we need a method of discernment for the normal person who does not have the gift of psychic sight, which enables some healers to see the Electromagnetic Body. The method I use I have named, *The Holographic Scanning Technique,* which is a three-part scanning technique. I developed a fourth Holographic Scanning Method, which I call *The Flat-Handed Scanning Method*. All you need are your own two hands and an open mind. If you are inexperienced in Energy Medicine, start by rubbing your hands together for a few minutes to wake up the chakras that exist in the palms of your hands, and then follow the below instructions.

THE HOLOGRAPHIC SCANNING TECHINQUE:

I will teach you how to sense, feel, scan and intuit the Aura or The Electromagnetic Body. Many use the word, Aura, and Electromagnetic Body interchangeably, because it is a simplified version of The Electromagnetic Body and more people know about the word, *Aura.* I will teach you how to scan the Aura/Electromagnetic Body by way of a holographic image that God will instruct his angels to put up for you. All that is required is faith in God and an open mind..

I recommend that you get permission from The Father before attempting to work on anyone. You do this by asking, *Father, should I work on this person?* Wait for a yes or no answer. If you cannot hear this answer, feel it with your gut. How do you feel? Are you drawn to continue or do you feel like you should not? Just do not let fear get in your way because this is your first attempt in working with the Electromagnetic Body and God. My suggestion is that you and a friend or loved one try this experiment together. This is a good way to feel comfortable in your first attempt in a Energy Medicine healing session. In addition, it is universal law that you need permission to work on anyone or even read anyone on a psychic basis. Otherwise, it is a manipulation of their free will, which is forbidden by God, since he granted us all *free will.*

Let us get started by learning the scanning procedure in order to ascertain what healing work needs to be done. You will use the scanning technique for almost every technique. That is until you get to the advanced healers level, of having psychic vision and/or hearing. In order to receive these great gifts, you must pray to God and ask God for these great gifts. If God decides to grant you these great gifts, it usually takes several years for them to manifest in the physical.

The easiest way to run a healing session is to have a person reclining on a massage table with a pillow under their knees. This is for their comfort, and your comfort, since a massage table is at table height, and you do not need to be in a constant bending-over stance, which has the potential to strain your back. However, in a pinch a sofa, bed, or chair can be used for the client. If you are comfortable with the person or client, another way with *direct contact* is to sit facing the client in a chair. Place your palms over the back of their hands while their hands rest, palms down, on their knees. This enables the energy to go into the back of the clients palm chakras. Since it is direct contact, this speeds up the flow of the energy. You should not run energy longer than twenty or thirty minutes when you first get started in healing work, as longer than this has the potential to tire you. Breaks should be taken in between clients or people you are working on. In which time you should clear yourself with the Energetic Hygiene Prayer. Additionally, you should eat some protein like nuts, drink some milk or have some chocolate.

Once you have discerned where the healing work needs to be done by the below scanning method, you will then hold your hands a few inches above the persons body while you send the energy to the area that you can feel is afflicted. Many times, the healing energy will put the person to sleep or they will need to sleep once they get home.

There should be a wait of a least a week, in between sessions, in order for the healing energy to assimilate. *Each time you run a session, you must check steps one through five in order, before moving onto the next technique.* I also recommend that you advice the client not to have any other type of energy work done during your work together as this will disrupt the frequency and vibration of the work you have done.

HOLOGRAPHIC SCANNING PROCEDURES:

1. Scan the <u>outside</u> of the aura in a circle to see what needs to be repaired or removed by asking, Father, is there anything not for (my/their/his/her/etc.)_____highest good that needs to be removed?

2. Scan the <u>front and back</u> of the body as though a person is turned sideways, by drawing an imaginary figure of a human body in front of you, about the size of a doll. Ask Father, is there anything not for (my/their/his/her/etc.)_____highest good that needs to be removed, on the front and back of (my/their/his/her/etc.)_____body?

3. Scan the <u>left and the right</u> sides of the person, as though they are facing you, by drawing an imaginary figure of a human body, in front of you about the size of a doll. Ask Father, is there anything not for (my/their/his/her/etc.)_____highest good, that needs to be removed, on the left or right side of (my/their/his/her/etc.)_____ body? See diagrams on the next few pages.

YATUVAY FLAT-HANDED HOLOGRAPHIC SCANNING METHOD:

The easiest way to assess the mental and emotional balancing techniques is to use what I call a flat-handed holographic scan. This is a very easy Holographic Scanning Technique. Picture moving your hand over an invisible flat line or surface, and you will feel that Gods angels have put up a firm, holographic, energetic line that will feel like two bumps. If the two bumps are even, then you are being show that there is a good balance, and that the technique is unnecessary. If you find a large bump and a small bump, this illustrates that the balance is way off. Additionally, this is a good way to get a yes or no answer. A yes answer is a big bump, and a no answer will show you a total flat line. *See below scan for practice.* See illustration on the following pages. *However, before using any of these scanning methods, you must utilize the prayers for Energetic Hygiene.*

YATUVAY PRAYER FOR USING A FLAT-HANDED HOLOGRAPHIC SCAN:

To get a yes or not answer using this scan, say: Father, please show me by way of flat-handed, holographic scan, (ask your question),_____for a yes or no answer.

In all of these steps, you will soon feel an energy that has been projected, in front of you that you can feel with the palm of your hand. This energy is a holograph that God has instructed your angels to create for you. It may take a few tries and a little practice to feel the energy the first time. Further, you can say; *please, make the energy stronger so that I can feel it or please, make the holograph a little smaller or larger.* You should be looking for a holograph that is roughly the size of a two-foot tall doll. Set your intention on the holographic image of the scan as though it were two feet in height and width. The goal is so that you can scan from the top of the head, to the bottom of the feet. Most people when first getting started with the scanning methods, attempt to feel the holograph as though it is a full-sized person instead of a holograph. Remember that you are looking for a holographic image that is only about two feet high.

STEP ONE ~ ENERGETIC HYGIENE:

Not to be redundant, but I need to reiterate the importance of this message, *before you begin any healing work, both you and the person you plan on working on must be cleared. This is the very first step you must take in any session and the one-step that can never be skipped.*

There are many energies that are not for your highest good that become attached to your bodies from the astral dimensions. I am sure that you have previously heard of such things as energy vampires that drain your energy. Who needs this problem? By using the prayer listed below, you will find that almost all energies that are not for your highest good, will be removed by God. You will then experience feeling so much lighter, happier and more peaceful, than you have ever felt in your entire life. Additionally, the prayer not only removes astral energies but also neutralizes viruses and bacteria so that you do not catch other people's germs in the energy exchange. You can also use this prayer if you get the flu or have any other type of illness. If the illness is chronic, it will take many sessions to neutralize the germs, and then is followed by The Cellular Release Technique. I usually pray prior to any healing work and like to use, *The Lord's Prayer and The Hail Mary,* as part of my normal procedure. These prayers are to show honor to God, in both his masculine and feminine qualities for the love, grace, mercy and assistance in our healing session and lives. However, you may use any prayer or free form of prayer that you wish when you make contact with God. I have modified the Hail Mary a little. I list these prayers

THE LORDS PRAYER
Our Father Who Art in Heaven
Hallowed be Thy Name
Thy Kingdom come,
Thy Will be done,
On Earth as it is in Heaven,
Give us this day our daily bread,
And forgive us our trespasses,
As we forgive those who trespass against us,
And lead us not into temptation,
But deliver us from all evil,
For Thy Art the Kingdom,
the Power and the Glory forever more.
Amen
HAIL MARY
Hail Mary, full of grace,
The Lord is with thee,
Blessed are thou amongst women,
And Blessed are thy the Fruit of thy Womb, Jesus,
Holy Mary, Mother of God,
Pray for us sinners at the hour of our death,
And assist us in our work today.
Amen

YATUVAY ENERGETIC HYGIENE PRAYER:

(This prayer should be said aloud on a *daily basis* to keep your systems clear and clean. This will only take a couple of minutes) Say:

We send energy to You, Father, in the vibration of unconditional love and ask in the Name of Jesus Christ, that You send the energy back to facilitate the work we are doing here today.

We ask Your Holy Spirit to place protection around us, and in our sphere of influence, for a period of ten days. We also ask that filters be placed in our cords, palms and feet chakras.

We ask that You send the vibration of Viral/Bacteria Neutralization to neutralize any virus/bacteria or illness in our bodies, and in the clearing vibration for the length of time that is appropriate for each of us.

We ask You, Father, in the Name of Jesus Christ, to remove all dark beings and energies that are not for our highest good, from our bodies and sphere of influence in all worlds, all dimensions, wherever and whenever. Thy Will be done. Amen.

Now you will start utilizing the Holographic Scanning Methods. However, there is another deeper level of clearing work, in which a programmed crystal is necessary for use in the clearing work. To explain why this is, let me tell you what the crystal adds to the clearing or healing work. What crystals simply do is they amplify your energy. In this case, the crystal amplifies your energy, enabling the removal of other stronger, darker energies. This is the reason why crystals have been used for centuries to run our wristwatches. They contain energy that runs the watch. Crystals are the *storers* of energy. Another way that crystals are used in YATUVAY healing sessions is to *store the vibration of love* in it or other energy program, to send love to God in gratitude, and to others who need love. I highly recommend that you consider getting these crystals for the deeper levels of clearing. If you decide you would like to order these very special crystals, please see Adolphina's website at www.AdolphinaShephard.com. In the Scanning procedures below, you will feel a buzzing or tingling in your fingertips and palm chakras. This feeling can feel hot, it could feel very cold, or you may feel it as a big bump or little bump. Everyone feels these things slightly differently. The key is to be alert for a subtle, energetic sensation.

HOLOGRAPHIC SCANNING PROCEDURES FOR ENERGETIC HYGIENE:

1. Scan the outside of the aura in a circle to see what needs to be removed by asking "Father, is there anything not for (my/their/his/her/etc.)_____highest good that needs to be removed?

2. Scan the front and back of the body as though a person is turned sideways, by drawing an imaginary figure of a human body in front of you, about the size of a doll. Ask Father; is there anything not for (my/their/his/her/etc.)_____highest good that needs to be removed, on the front and back of____body?

3. Scan the left and the right sides of the person, as though they are facing you, by drawing an imaginary figure of a human body, in front of you about the size of a doll. Ask Father, is there anything not for (my/their/his/her/etc.)_____highest good, that needs to be removed, on the left or right side of the body? See diagrams on the next few pages.

STEP TWO ~ THE GRID SYSTEM:

The second step is to repair the Grid System. This is because everyone, and I mean everyone, on whom I have ever worked, has had a multitude of holes in their Grid System, eventually leading to ill health. Imagine filling up a balloon with oxygen. If there are holes in the balloon, no matter how much oxygen you put into the balloon, it will never stay inflated. This is the same with the Electromagnetic Body. *The Aura must be tightly sealed.* Otherwise, the energy will just continue to flow out through the breaks and holes, which then leads to an ineffective repair session.

The Grid System is part of and encompassed in your Aura or Electromagnetic Body. Your Aura is shaped like a big balloon that is full of air, with grid lines that look similar to a fish netting, that completely surround the Aura. Furthermore, grids are what hold your Aura or Electromagnetic Body together in this series of interconnecting threads. Additionally, there are other aspects to the Grid System. Your Grid System connects to the meridians of the body. Thus, the grids are on the outside of the physical body and the meridians are on the inside of the body. Grids also connect you to other dimensions.

Each layer of your Electromagnetic Body connects with a chakra, and connects with a dimension. Each person should have in place, at least seven strong grids layers, to work in harmony with the seven main chakras. However, most people are only functioning on a three-grid system, which is due to damage to their system. When there are holes in the Grid System, a person will obviously not be able to function at their peak, as the heart must work very hard to keep the electromagnetic energy flowing around the body, since this energy is our very life-force itself. Therefore, the Grid System must be in good working order for a person to maintain good health. I suspect that many heart attacks and syndromes like Chronic Fatigue Syndrome and/or Fibromyalgia, are a result of having holes in the Grid System. There are always holes in the Grid System in the beginning sessions. Run this segment of the healing session for fifteen minutes. To assess for holes in the Grid System, you must say:

YATUVAY PRAYER FOR GRID REPAIR

We send energy to You, Father, in the vibration of unconditional love and ask in the Name of Jesus Christ, that You send the energy back to facilitate the work we are doing here today.

We ask Your Holy Spirit to place protection around us, and in our sphere of influence, for a period of ten days. We also ask that filters be placed in our cords, palms and feet chakras.

Please send your Holy Spirit to repair any holes in (my/their/his/her/etc.)_____Grid System in all worlds, all dimensions, whatever, wherever that are appropriate, that (my/their/his/her/etc.)_____be made whole and healthy. We thank You for the healing, the Light and Your protection. Thy Will be done. Amen.

HOLOGRAPHIC SCANNING PROCEDURES FOR GRID REPAIR:

To assess for holes in the Grid System, say:

Father, please show me if there are any holes in (my/their/his/her/etc.)_____Grid System? Then scan the aura to feel, sense or see if there are any holes in the Grid System".

1. Scan the outside of the aura in a circle to see what needs to be repaired by asking Father, are there holes in (my/their/his/her/etc.) _____body that needs to be repaired?

2. Scan the front and back of the body as though a person is turned sideways by drawing an imaginary figure of a human body in front of you, about the size of a doll. Ask Father, are there any holes in the Grid System that needs to be repaired on the front and back of (my/their/his/her/etc.) _____body?

3. Scan the left and the right sides of a person, as though they are facing you by drawing an imaginary figure of a human body in front of you about the size of a doll. Ask Father, is there anything that needs to be repaired on the left or right side of (my/their/his/her/etc.)_____ body?

THIRD STEP-UNBLOCKING THE CHAKRAS

The third step is to unblock and repair the chakras. Otherwise, pushing energy through blocked chakras could blow a hole in the chakras, and more holes in the Grid System. The simplified chakra system consists of seven main chakras. Think of them as spinning wheels of energy that send energy throughout your body. You may picture that the chakras look like an ice cream cone, which are centered, front to back through your torso. The larger ends of the ice cream cones are in the front of your torso, from the top of your head, to the bottom of your torso.

There are chakras above your head extending into infinity (activated as far as you are on a spiritual basis) and below the feet. There are hundreds of secondary chakras that assist to run your body, but we are only going to focus on the seven primary chakras listed below at this time.

1. The crown chakra-Top of head-color-white
2. The 3rd eye-Between the two eyes-color-indigo
3. The throat-The throat area-color-blue
4. The heart-In the center of your chest-color-pink/green
5. The solar plexus-Right around your belly button-color-yellow
6. The Sacral-Right below your belly button-color-orange
7. The Root-In the area of your pelvic bone-color red

The important thing to know about chakras is that they must not be blocked up. Our goal is to keep them unblocked at all times, so that the energy can flow throughout the entire body. You might liken a blocked chakra, to a sparkplug in a car that is not working well. Should there be a clogged sparkplug; the entire car does not run well. This is the same as with the body. To clear and balance the chakras, you will stand on the receiving persons' side, placing your sending hand over the front of the person's chakras. Then the receiving hand over the back of the persons chakras. (The sending hand is the hand you write with). Next, scan up and down their body for blocks or imbalances in the chakras keeping your hands about six inches away from the physical body.

The way that you can tell that a chakra is blocked, is when you cannot feel any energy flowing between the front and back of the body, between your hands. When the chakras are completely balanced, you will feel an energy that almost feels like a ping-pong ball bouncing back and forth between your hands. Front and back. Front and back again. There are times when the chakra block will be removed, and you will feel the ping-pong ball bouncing between your hands, then it will block up again. I almost feel this like a string of pearls being pulled out of the chakras. You should stay in the same area until you are certain that the string of pearls (blocks being removed) are completely removed, and you feel a strong bouncing back and forth of the energy. When the chakras are completely balanced, they will slide sideways, and you will feel a cyclical feeling between your hands. Now, you know you are done with clearing the chakras.

YATUVAY CHAKRA BALANCING PRAYER

Say: We send energy to You, Father, in the vibration of unconditional love and ask in the Name of Jesus Christ that You send the energy back to us to facilitate the work we are doing here today.

We ask for protection to be placed around (me/us/he/she/etc,)_____ and our sphere of influence, by Your Holy Spirit for a period of ten days. We ask that filters be placed in our cords, palm and feet chakras.

We ask You to send Your Holy Spirit to remove any blocks from (my/their/his/her/etc.)_____ chakras, to repair, and balance them in _____bodies in all worlds, all dimensions, wherever, whatever, that is appropriate. That (I/they/he/she/etc,)_____ be made whole and healthy. We thank You for the healing, the light and your protection. Thy Will be done. Amen".

HOLOGRAPHIC SCANNING PROCEDURES:

To assess if chakras need clearing and balancing,(they will need clearing and balancing), say:

Father, please show me where the imbalances or blocks are in (my/their/his/her/etc.)_____chakras? Then scan the aura to feel, sense, or see if there are any blocks or imbalances in the Chakra System. You must assess each of the seven primary chakras.

1. Scan the <u>front and back</u> of the body as though a person is turned sideways, by drawing an imaginary figure of a human body in front of you, about the size of a doll. Ask Father, is there anything not for (my/their/his/her/etc.)_____highest good that needs to be removed or repaired in (my/their/his/her,etc.) _____chakras? See diagrams on the next few pages.

FOURTH STEP: RUNNING A COOKIE AND SCAN DISC

The fourth step is to run a Cookie and Scan Disc. This will remove what I have termed cookies, negative thought forms, attachments, devices, implants, shackles, cords and all manner of things that cause ill health. These items can also prevent the client from moving forward in life, which keeps them living in the past. To give you an analogy of what I am talking about, think about how outdated cookies and programs slow down your computer. Every so often, it is necessary that you run a scan disc in order to clean up your computer, so that it runs efficiently. This same theory applies to the Electromagnetic Body. An average client needs ten to twenty sessions, timed about one month apart, to bring them up to full speed. If interspersed with other techniques, a little at a time for approximately ten to fifteen minutes, this should not put the client into overload. Alternatively, you can run one thirty or forty-minute session focusing on just this technique one time a month. You must run energetic hygiene first.

HOLOGRAPHIC SCANNING TECHNIQUE

1 CIRCLE *OUTSIDE* OF AURA

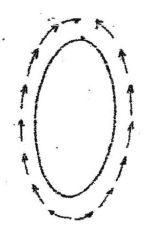

#2 SCANNING *INSIDE* OF AURA

FRONT   BACK

#3 SCANNING *INSIDE* OF AURA

LEFT   RIGHT

FLAT-HANDED HOLOGRAHIC SCAN

SCAN SHOWING IMBALANCE

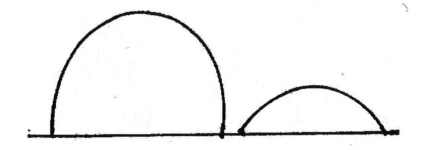

SCAN SHOWING BALANCE

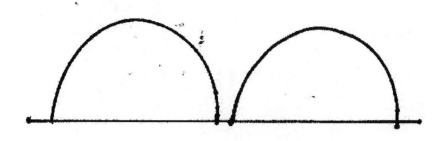

HOLOGRAPHIC SCANNING TECHNIQUE
FOR THE
THE SEVEN GRID CIRCULATORY SYSTEM
OF
THE ELECTROMAGNETIC BODY

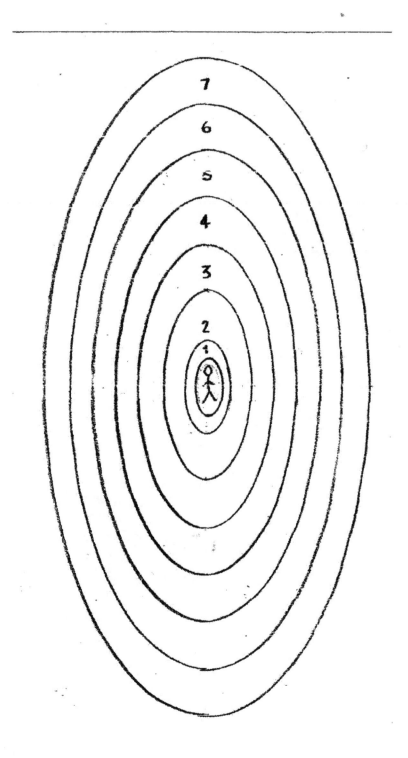

THE BASIC CHAKRA SYSTEM

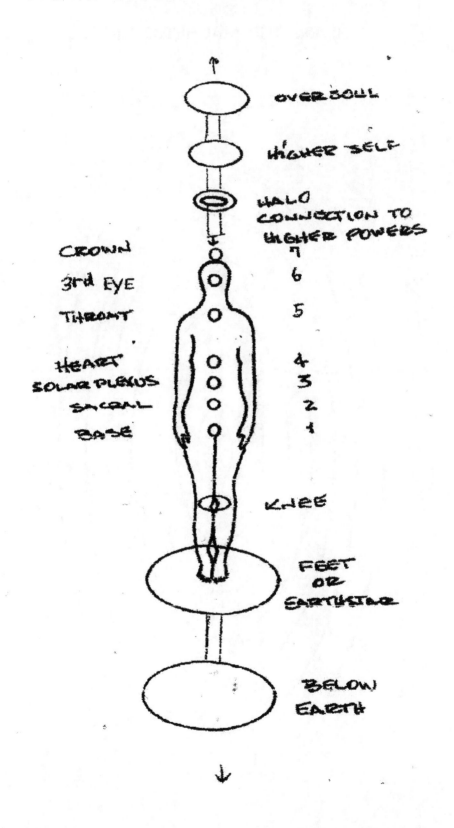

YATUVAY PRAYER FOR COOKIE & SCAN DISC: REMOVING COOKIES, NEGATIVE THOUGHT FORMS, CORDS, IMPLANTS AND OTHER OBJECTS

We send energy to You, Father, in the vibration of unconditional love and ask in the Name of Jesus Christ that You send the energy back to us, to facilitate the work we are doing today.

We ask for protection to be placed around us, and in our sphere of influence, by Your Holy Spirit, for a period of ten days. We ask that filters be put in our cords, palm and feet chakras.

We ask You to send Your Holy Spirit to remove cookies, negative thought forms, cords, implants and any other objects, which are not for (my/their/his/hers etc.)_____highest good, that can safely be removed today, in priority order in all worlds, all dimensions, wherever, whatever that are appropriate. That they be made whole and healthy.

We thank You for the healing, the light and your protection, Lord God. Thy Will be done! Amen.

HOLOGRAPHIC SCANNING TECHNIQUE:

Father, please show me if there are any items that should be removed by running a Cookie and Scan Disc session for (my/their/his/her/etc.)_____. You must scan to feel, sense or see, if there are any items that should be removed by Cookie and Scan Disc. You must assess first by using all three scans, as well as, checking each seven primary chakras. Run this segment about ten minutes each time you run a healing session.

1. Scan the outside of the aura in a circle to see what needs to be removed by asking Father, is there anything not for (my/their/his/her/etc.) _____highest good and greatest expansion that needs to be removed?

2. Scan the front and back of the body as though a person is turned sideways by drawing an imaginary figure of a human body in front of you, about the size of a doll. Ask Father; is there anything that needs to be removed, on the front and back of (my/their/his/her/etc.) _____body?

3. Scan the left and the right sides of a person, as though they are facing you by drawing an imaginary figure of a human body in front of you about the size of a doll. Ask Father, is there anything that needs to be removed on the left or right side of (my/their/his/her/etc.)_____ body.

FIFTH STEP-MERIDIAN REPAIR:

The fifth step is to repair the Meridian System. Since the meridians feed our nervous system and our organs, right down to the very cellular structure, it is extremely important to keep the meridians intact. All of our organs have a limited life span and must be fed energy in order to live a healthy, long life. Let me give you an example. Suppose the heart meridian has breaks in it or is broken. What this means is that the heart is not being fed the energy to support its function. This forces the heart to live off of it own energy source, instead of the energy that God sends to us every second, of every minute, of every day, to sustain us. Within a fairly short timeframe, the heart will become very tired, and the person will most likely suffer heart challenges. This is one of the major reasons a person has the potential to experience a heart attack. The heart is just simply overworked and exhausted. Along with clogged arteries, this creates a situation, in which someone has a greater potential to experience a heart attack. The heart meridian is not the only repair that is generally needed when a person has heart challenges, but is a very important step. Cording cutting is another major step, as the cords emanate from the heart, and have a tendency to strangle the heart. Refer to the Manual Section to see more. However, not everyone can repair Meridians, unless they have the Gift of the Holy Spirit, given to them by God. Therefore, this technique can be a hit or miss repair until someone reaches this level of service to God.

YATUVAY MERIDIAN REPAIR PRAYERS:

We send energy to You, Father, in the vibration of unconditional love and ask in the Name of Jesus Christ that You send the energy back to us, to facilitate the work we are doing today.

We ask for protection to be placed around us, and our sphere of influence, by Your Holy Spirit, for a period of ten days. We ask for filters to be placed in our cords, our palm and feet chakras.

We ask You to send Your Holy Spirit to repair any breaks or blocks in our meridians in (my/their/his/her/ etc.)_____body, in priority order, in all worlds, all dimensions, wherever, whatever, that is appropriate. That (I/they/he/she/we/etc.)____ be made whole and healthy. We thank You for the healing, the Light and Your protection, Lord God. Thy Will be done! Amen.

HOLOGRAPHIC SCANNING TECHNIQUE:

1. Scan the outside of the aura in a circle to see what needs to be repaired by asking Father, is there any meridian in (my/their/his/her/etc.) _____body that needs to be repaired?

2. Scan the front and back of the body as though a person is turned sideways by drawing an imaginary figure of a human's body in front of you, about the size of a doll. Father, is there any meridians that need repair on the front and back of (my/their/his/her/etc.) _____body?

3. Scan the left and the right sides of a person, as though they are facing you by drawing an imaginary figure of a human's body in front of you about the size of a doll. Ask Father, is there any meridian that needs repair on the left or right side of (my/their/his/her/etc.)_____ body?

SIXTH STEP: BUILDING THE STRENGTH OF THE ELECTROMAGNETIC BODY

The sixth step is to continue to perform the previous five techniques for approximately ten sessions. This is required in order to build the strength of the Electromagnetic Body in you or your client. These ten sessions, should be done at least a week apart, in order for the healing to assimilate. It is important to inform the client that it is not in their best interest to have any other energy work done by any other practitioner during the period that the two of you are working together. This would disrupt the healing that is occurring by disrupting the frequency and vibration that is currently processing. *The first several sessions are to be focused only on clearing negative energies, repairing the grids, and clearing the chakras. After three sessions, you may proceed to add the scan disc for several sessions, before attempting to move on to the meridians.* These multiple sessions will assist in raising your frequency before attempting the meridian repair process. Use previously listed prayers. Then it is time for the seventh step.

SEVENTH STEP: STRIKING LEVEL I

The seventh step is to perform the Striking I technique. What this Striking Technique does, is to clear out of the entire body, all the goo that has accumulated in your entire system. To give you an idea of what I mean, I want you to picture that you walk through an electromagnetic dust storm, and that the dust cannot help but be absorbed by our energy system, which is twirling with energy all of the time. The striking removes the goo that you have absorbed your entire life, starting with the prana tube to the chakras. Then on to the chakras through to the meridians. The next step is clearing the nervous system. Striking then clears out the organs. Next, Striking will clean the blood and finally, the cellular structure. Now, your cells can carry more light, which will raise your frequency and vibration.

Another way to think of the subject of Striking, is to drive a car for 200,000 thousand miles and not change the oil. The oil filter becomes clogged, and can no longer filter the dirty oil, which results in clogging the car engine. Thus, the car no longer runs well. This same result occurs with the Electromagnetic Body absorbing the electromagnetic dust from birth. We are continually bombarded with electromagnetic frequencies, from all electrical and wireless devices starting with our television set, the microwave, computers, and our refrigerators. One of the worst electromagnetic frequencies that we are all exposed to is our wireless technology.

There is not another technique that exists that can clear out the entire body in one session. The Lord God gave this technique to me, to assist humanity. It is unknown in this day, this age, except to those that I have trained to perform this technique. It is truly a very effective technique. After the Striking has taken place, a person will continue to purge and clear for about six months through their finger and toe meridians. After the body has become clear of all of the electromagnetic slug and goo, the client or patient will have much more energy. Additionally, as this occurs, the Physical Body's very frequency and vibration will rise, triggering a rise in the person's consciousness, leading them to enlightenment. This greatly assists someone in his or her evolutionary process. Unfortunately, this technique is a *unique hands-on technique that* must be taught in a class setting. Therefore, I am unable to give you further details in this book. If you are interested in learning this technique, you may access Adolphina's website to see when and where this class is being taught.

However, it is a prerequisite in order to take this particular class, that you have been following the above six steps for at least ten sessions. This is to make sure that your system is up to the task, and can handle the Striking Method. Otherwise, there is the potential for damage to be created, rather than repaired, to the Electromagnetic Body by this step which is performed in group hands-on practice. After the seventh step, it is time to start enhancing the Electromagnetic Body, using a variety of different techniques that will correct many illnesses or injuries in the Physical Body, as a secondary result, of the repairs made to the Electromagnetic Body. Of course, the technique that is used will be determined by the client's illness or injury.

The following techniques that I am about to teach you, are ones that will greatly assist you and your clients. Please bear in mind that the Energy Medicine Techniques given in this book are a much shorter version than what a workshop would entail. However, I want to give you as much help and knowledge that I can, without creating a book that is three thousand pages long. I have personally experienced all of these techniques that I have either learned and/or that have been given by God, and now will share them with you.

I will teach you three important techniques that have the potential to balance the Mental Body and the Emotional Body. I have decided to share these particular techniques because of all of the fear and angst that I can feel that humanity is going through, as a result of the current recession, with their resulting financial concerns. Of course, there are many other reasons why someone may be unbalanced that these techniques will assist with greatly.

Some of the emotional balancing tools that are used in YATUVAY are, Yin/Yang Balancing, Emotional Balancing & Transmutation, and Blueprint Restoration. These techniques are all extremely powerful, and work in different areas of the brain, the solar plexus, the ovaries, the testes and, our primal brain, which lies in the abdomen area.

These emotional balancing techniques should be done on separate dates. Otherwise, you or the client could go on energetic overload, and feel emotionally overwhelmed. If all techniques are done at one time, there may also be dizziness as the brain and emotions try to balance in one felt swoop. Therefore, I recommended that no more than two of these techniques be done in any healing session. The difference that you will see in you or your client's emotional equilibrium, after running any of these emotional or mental balancing techniques is so astounding, that it is impossible to describe. It is something that you just have to witness. The timelines are in Chapter 7.

It is important to understand that the number of sessions necessary will be determined by the spiritual strength, frequency, and vibration of the Energy Medicine Practitioner's Electromagnetic Body, and by how badly damaged, and weakened the client's Electromagnetic, Mental, Emotional and Physical Bodies are. Sometimes, it can take just a few sessions and sometimes it is necessary to have a weekly or bi-monthly session for six months. However, all of these techniques require a minimum wait between sessions of at least a day or more. Some techniques can only be run one time a month or every three months because they are so very powerful.

YIN/YANG BALANCING:

Yin and Yang are a binary system built upon the two most basic energies of the entire universe, which are yin and yang. Yin, is associated with water and earth is the receptive, yielding, nurturing aspect of the universe and the feminine creative principle of gestation. Yin is in the mysteries, the strength of flexibility, adaptation, patience and endurance. Conversely, yang is the masculine creative energy of initiation, fixed, forceful aggressive and dominating. Yang is embodied in fire and air and heat. Yin yields and permits, yang pushes forward and stands firm. Both are present *in all that exists and are equally crucial to universal equilibrium.* The constant shifts and changes in our world, the entire cosmos, and indeed, us, reflect the ongoing give and take between these polarized energies. I found this explanation of Yin/Yang and adapted it from a wonderful little book called, (The Lost Art of I Ching, by Peter Pauper Press, Inc.)

Additionally, Yin/Yang represent the two sides of the coin, such as; the balance of the head and heart, thought and compassion, male and female, the light and the dark in each person, duality versus polarity and integration. This technique will not only resolve many emotional challenges, but will also assist in bringing peace to the world. One time is all that is needed to balance the Yin/Yang, but an emotionally upsetting event can cause the Yin/Yang equilibrium to swing out of balance again. When this happens, the client may experience extremes in emotions such as anger, fear, sadness, clinging, etc. Yin/Yang Balancing can be done as often as needed.

It is an extremely fearful time right now for many people, with the ongoing recession and with so many being out of work. We all have a lot of buried sub-conscious fear from our many lifetimes, where we have died through some type of trauma, or experienced trauma in some other fashion such as war.

However, *we must learn to not let fear rule us, we must rule fear.* This is an extremely important concept. Yin/Yang Balancing is the answer in overcoming fear, along with the other emotional and mental techniques, in establishing peace in our hearts. When we establish peace in our own heart, this offers peace to others and helps them to experience healing in their own heart.

Overcoming fear is one of the reasons why this technique is so very important in maintaining emotional balance. Please use it often.

The right side of the body is Yang and the left side of the body is Yin. If you or a client has, a physical challenge that exists, on either side of the body, Yin/Yang Balancing can be used to assist in resolving this challenge. This imbalance between the Yin/Yang is what has allowed to world to fall into constant war instead of peace. Whenever you or a client feels overly stressed, check and see if the Yin/Yang balance is off. The easiest way to assess this is with a flat-handed holographic scan. You will feel two bumps. If the bumps are even, they are balanced. If you find a large bump and a small bump, this illustrates that the Yin/Yang is out of balance. It has been my personal experience that every single person needs to have balanced regularly, especially, until Inner Child Work is completed. Remember to use it often for any emotional or mental imbalance.

YATUVAY PRAYER FOR YIN/YANG BALANCING:

We send energy to You, Father, in the vibration of unconditional love and ask in the Name of Jesus Christ that You send the energy back to us to facilitate the work we are doing today.

We ask for protection to be placed around us, and our sphere of influence, by Your Holy Spirit, for a period of ten days. We ask for filters to be put in our cords, palm and feet chakras.

We ask You to send Your Holy Spirit to balance our Yin/Yang energies in all worlds, all dimensions, wherever, whatever that are appropriate.

That (my/they/his/her/etc.)_____ be made whole and healthy. We thank You for the healing, the Light and Your protection, Lord God. Thy Will be done! Amen.

YATUVAY FLAT-HANDED SCANNING METHOD:

Father, please show me (my/their/his/her/etc.)_____ Yin/Yang Balance.

Continue to check by scanning for when the Yin/Yang is balanced which will be represented by two even bumps.

EMOTIONAL BALANCING AND TRANSMUTATION:

This self-explanatory technique is very useful when feeling stressed out. In fact, one of the ways you can tell that you or your client emotions are out of balance, are when you are stressed. Having angry or tearful outbursts, slamming things or sinking into a depression are all signs that your emotions need to be balanced. However, once your emotions are balanced, any emotionally upsetting event can cause the Emotional Balancing & Transmutation balance to fall off its equilibrium. One session will normally do the trick, but it can slip out of balance due to any trauma or emotionally upsetting event. Emotional Balancing & Transmutation is a tool that can and should be used as needed. Emotional balancing works strictly by balancing and transmuting the emotions.

YATUVAY PRAYER FOR EMOTIONAL BALANCING AND TRANSMUTATION:

We send energy to You, Father, in the vibration of unconditional love and ask in the Name of Jesus Christ that You send the energy back to us to facilitate the work we are doing today.

We ask for protection to be placed around us, and our sphere of influence, by Your Holy Spirit, for a period of ten days. We ask for filters to be put in our cords, palm and feet chakras.

We ask You to send Your Holy Spirit to balance our emotions and transmute any harmful emotions into love in all worlds, all dimensions, wherever, whatever, that are appropriate.

That (me/their/he/she/etc.)_____ is made whole and healthy. We thank You for the healing, the Light and Your protection, Lord God. Thy Will be done! Amen.

YATUVAY FLAT-HANDED SCANNING METHOD:

Father, please show me (my/their/his/her/etc.)_____ emotional balance..

Continue to check the emotional balance by scanning until you find two even bumps.

BLUEPRINT RESTORATION:

This is an advanced class. However, with seeing the signs of people going crazy everywhere, as viewed everyday on television or in the newspapers, I have decided to release this information for other advanced Energy Medicine Metaphysicians. To fully assess the Blueprint, you need psychic vision in order to use this technique. Otherwise, you must use Holographic Scan number one, repeatedly. During the time you are using this technique, you must check every couple of minutes. Do not run this technique for more than ten minutes at a time.

Blueprint Restoration takes our Spiritual Bodies back to the perfect formatting that it was when God created it. Through misuse of our free will, given to us by God, our Blueprint can become distorted and unbalanced. Which then results in an imbalance of all of our bodies, and can result in serious mental illness. Blueprint Restoration typically takes several months to fully assimilate, and to restore wholeness. This technique is extremely powerful and should only be run every couple of months. Generally, two sessions are required to bring wholeness and harmony back to the individual. However, each person needs to be individually assessed until the Blueprint is restored to its perfect balance.

Do you remember the Slinky Toy? This is a simple toy made that resembles an interconnecting series of circles that allows this toy, to climb down the stairs all by itself. It has delighted children for decades. For visualization purposes, I want you to think of the Slinky, sitting in an upright position. This top view resembles what the Blueprint should look like. In the case of Blueprint Restoration, all of the circular parts that make up the Slinky are all bent out of shape, and twisted into various lumps, bumps, and other weird distortions. Using your psychic vision, as the original Blueprint falls back into place, you will see the entire group of circular parts losing its distortions, becoming round, and sliding back into one big, perfectly balanced circle. This balancing will continue to occur until it looks like one big circle. Alternatively, using scan number one, continue to repeat the scan, until you can feel only a completely round circle, with no distortions. When you feel only a round circle, you will know that the blueprint work has been completed. After ten minutes if the Blueprint is not finalized into one big circle, you will need to redo a Blueprint Restoration Healing Session in two months. You will see a complete transformation in the client, from being mentally off balance to mental balance in a few months time.

YATUVAY PRAYER FOR BLUEPRINT RESTORATION:

We send energy to You, Father, in the vibration of unconditional love and ask in the Name of Jesus Christ that You send the energy back to us to facilitate the work we are doing today.

We ask for protection to be placed around us, and our sphere of influence, by Your Holy Spirit, for a period of ten days. We ask for filters to be put in our cords, palm and feet chakras.

We ask You to send Your Holy Spirit to bring back into perfect form and balance, our original blueprint that you created, that (my/they/he/she/etc.)_____ be made whole and healthy. So that (I/they/he/she/ etc.)_____ may become who you intended me to be when You created me, in all worlds, all dimensions, wherever, whatever, that is appropriate. We thank You for the healing, the Light and your protection, Lord God. Thy Will be done! Amen.

HOLOGRAPHIC SCANNING PROCEDURE:

1. Scan the outside of the aura in a circle to see what needs to be repaired in the Blueprint by asking, Father, please show me (my/their/his/her/etc),_____ blueprint balance at this time and what needs to be repaired.

The techniques listed below, are highly advanced techniques that cannot easily be taught, or without in-depth training in a class. Following, you will find a general description of these advanced techniques.

- Chemical Balancing-The Chemical Balancing Technique restores perfect chemical balancing in our bodies, which has the potential to resolve all types of diseases from
- depression, diabetes, etc.
- Transmuting Our Karma Into Grace-Many times, people experience traumas and harsh lessons as a result of actions they have taken in this life and previous lives. By transmuting our karma into grace, we have the potential to resolve many challenges before they even take place.
- Compassion Technique-Enables the opening and expansion of our hearts enabling peace and harmony to come into existence, for we can now *feel* what others are feeling when our hearts are open, leading us to treat others as we want to be treated.
- Retrieving Our Soul Pieces-Throughout our many lifetimes, we have lost innumerable pieces of our soul through various traumas. These missing soul pieces are the key to why some people never feel whole or happy. By restoring these missing soul pieces, this will bring a person into wholeness.
- Filling Our Gas Tank-We have a storage tank of energy that needs to be refilled periodically, because when it gets close to empty, this is when death occurs. This technique along with a few other techniques, I have labeled, *The Fountain of Youth Series.*
- Recharging Our Batteries-This is a self-explanatory technique, and is another part of *The Fountain of Youth Series* that restores health and zest back into our lives.
- Sending and Receiving Forgiveness-Many illnesses are a result of *unforgiveness* in this life and other lifetimes. However, the forgiveness that I am talking about is not always about forgiving others, but the forgiveness of self. This technique is too powerful for words.
- Repairing Our DNA-This technique is self-explanatory. It has the potential to repair our damaged DNA. This is an advanced unique hands-on technique, which must be taught in person in its fullness.
- Repairing The Crystal System-We all have a Crystal System in our bodies, which for the most part, is not completely turned on, until your body can handle the surge. There usually are many broken crystals that cause an untold amount of pain, such as pain in the back, knees, elbows but can be anywhere in the body. This is an advanced Class.
- Spinal Energy Medicine-This is a unique hands-on technique that must be taught in class, but has the potential to repair herniated discs, and many other back disorders, including the *potential* to assist someone who may be paralyzed due to spinal cord damage get back their mobility.
- Repairing the Endocrine System-This is a self-explanatory technique that utilizes a unique hands-on technique that must be taught in person
- Healing Our Inner Child- Inner Child works by releasing and transmuting the negative emotions

that are held in the subconscious mind, such as fear, anger, grief, and abandonment. Inner Child is so powerful that this technique can only be done once every three months. This advanced powerful technique must be taught in its fullness.

- Repairing and/or Replacing The Etheric Organs-Self-explanatory technique that is extremely advanced technique and involves a unique hands-on technique that must be taught in its fullness.

If you are interested, you can check out Adolphina's website for a complete listing of classes that are available via a Virtual School or a workshop that might not be listed in this book at www. AdolphinaShephard.com.

CHAPTER 6 ~

Sacred Geometry & What Do We Do Now?

SACRED GEOMETRY:

As the Electromagnetic Body is repaired, and upgraded, it will start to change its *very shape*, which results in something that is called Sacred Geometry. Webster's Dictionary describes the word, *geometry*, as:

1. A branch of mathematics dealing with shapes.

Further, Webster's Dictionary defines the word, *sacred*, as:

1. Holy.

2. Secured against violation.

I am no expert in Geometry by any means so I did a little research on the internet in order to give you more detail. I found a website called: *The Sacred Landscape,* by Catherine Yronwode, from which I quote the following:

Sacred geometry is used by archaeologists, anthropologists, and geometricians to encompass the religious, philosophical, and spiritual beliefs that have sprung up around geometry in various cultures during the course of human history. It is a catchall term covering Pythagorean geometry, and neo-Platonic geometry, as well as the perceived relationships between organic curves and logarithmic curves. Here are a few examples of how the word, sacred, *has entered into geometry in different eras and cultures:*

1) The ancient Greeks assigned various attributes to the Platonic solids and to certain geometrically derived ratios, investing them with "meaning." For example, the cube symbolized kingship and earthly foundations, while the Golden Section was seen as a dynamic principle embodying philosophy and wisdom. Thus a building dedicated to a god-king might bear traces of cubic geometry, while one dedicated to a heavenly god might have been constructed using Golden Section proportions.

2) When Hindus (ancient and modern) plan to erect any edifice for religious purposes, from a small wayside shrine to an elaborate temple, they first perform a simple geometric construction on the ground, establishing due East and West and constructing a square there from. Upon this diagram, they lay out the entire building. The making of this geometric construction is accompanied by prayers and other religious observances.

3) The Christian religion uses the cross as its major religious emblem, and in geometric terms, this was elaborated upon during the medieval period, to the form of an unfolded cube (reminiscent of example #1 above, where the cube was equated with kingship). Many Gothic cathedrals were built using proportions derived from the geometry inherent in the cube and double-cube; this tradition continues in modern Christian churches to the present time.

You can see how the ancients in many cultures, used Sacred Geometry, and how deeply entrenched it is, in the manner in which buildings are still being constructed today, in our churches, temples and other buildings around the world. The cross is still used today in the Christian religions. However, in modern life except for those who study Sacred Geometry, very few people know anything about it. This just goes to show that there are very, deep, hidden, mysteries surrounding Sacred Geometry. This label, Sacred Geometry, is applied to many different shapes and symbols such as the crop circles you may have heard about on television or read about in the newspaper.

However, when am I referring to Sacred Geometry, I am referring to the *shape of the Electromagnetic Body. This is big news. The Electromagnetic Body changes its energetic shape, signature, and frequency, as a person further develops their Electromagnetic Body.* This has the wonderful side effect of expanding your consciousness. Perhaps, all of these ancient cultures understood that by growing your Electromagnetic Body that you become enlightened, which explains why these shapes were and still are so honored, and duplicated in buildings, churches and temples. Because by changing our Electromagnetic Body's shape, we reach the pinnacle of a *kingship unto ourselves.* These shapes can easily be assessed by utilizing The Holographic Scanning Methods. I have found from personal observation that the Electromagnetic Body changes its shape in the following order as a person grows in their body, mind and spirit: The shapes are listed as they occur in order.

A triangle	△
A diamond	◇
A cube	□
A star or merkaba	✳

This is a very simplified explanation, but I think you get the idea. If you are further interested, I would suggest searching the web. You will discover that as Sacred Geometry takes place that you will start to honor, and engage everyone through love, (even a bum in the street), losing judgment and your ego in the process.

WHAT DO WE DO NOW?

I have taught these techniques through a former modality called Ascension Healing. However, I have renamed Ascension Healing to, YATUVAY, after others reported finding other healers using the same name, but not the same techniques, frequency or vibration, thus causing confusion about this particular modality.

YATUVAY is a Name that has been given to me by our Creator to use for this particular modality. The Name "YATUVAY" was disclosed to me as a new Name of God. Additionally, I have been given a symbol for, YATUVAY, which is on the cover of this book in the upper right hand corner. This symbol represents the *Letter of The Mother*. This symbol was given to me four years ago, in preparation for this time, this age. YATUVAY is the 23rd missing letter of the Hebrew Alphabet, which represents that the world can now start to become whole. It has a numerical value of 1,000. This symbol represents *the marriage of the Divine Masculine and the Divine Feminine as an integrated whole*. Therefore, YATUVAY represents The Father, the Son and The Holy Spirit. The Holy Spirit holds the side of God that represents his feminine qualities.

There are many other names that I have heard God referred to such as, THE I AM THAT I AM, The Source, Prime Creator, The Central Sun, plus dozens of other names that exist. You may have also heard The Holy Spirit referred to as, The Shekinnah, or in ancient times, The Mother Goddess. The Lord, Jesus Christ, is birthed by a combination of The Father and The Mother qualities, so he embodies both masculine and feminine characteristics. When using the Modality of YATUVAY, you are experiencing the "Power of One" through The Holy Trinity. This is Energy Medicine at its highest pinnacle.

YATUVAY is often a life-changing experience, utilizing new frequencies, faith and prayer to allow for the healing of the Spiritual Bodies of the Electromagnetic Bodies and its sub-systems. This gives Adolphina the ability to have *The Power of One* with the Father and his Universes of angels, and you too, if God determines that this be so. Additionally, the methodology of the whole system of sending energy has been upgraded and changed. Whereas in the past, energy was sent directly to a client, now instead, the energy is sent, in the vibration of unconditional love, to God and God then facilitates the healing session. This gives us the ability to work with *The Power Of One* through God's good grace and mercy. *This is what makes the Modality of YATUVAY completely different from any other modality, as well as the use of prayer,* and laying-on-of-the-hands.

When first starting to work with Energy Medicine, usually one first starts by with working with their guardian angel. As they progress, they start working with Ascended Masters or Saints, who have mastered the qualities that, Jesus Christ, showed us when he was in the physical. The next promotion or step is then to work with, Jesus Christ, and his universes. Lastly, if you pass all the tests, that you are given each step of the way, you may be chosen to reach the pinnacle of working with directly with The Father and his universes. This is what is meant by the statement in the Bible that *you can only get to the Father through the*

Son! Some time ago, Adolphina reached this level, from working with The Son's Universe, Jesus Christ, to The Father and His Universes.

Therefore, the timing was right for YATUVAY at this moment in time and space. It is a blending of the Ascension Healings Modality and Techniques, and YATUVAY'S Energy, Love and Power. When we utilize the methodology of YATUVAY, *we are transcending time and space.* This is because *it is God, who is sending The Holy Trinity's Great Energy and Power, to accomplish our work.* This is what gives YATUVAY Practitioners, *The Power of One.* YATUVAY is the energy we have been waiting for. It is the purest form of energy from God. It is the Energy of the Masculine and the Feminine of God.

Stated from the book (The Oracle of Kabbalah) by Richard Seidman. *According to the book (The Oracle of Kabbalah,) there is a 13th century kabalistic text, (Sefer HaTemunah) (The Book of the Image) teaches that one letter is missing from the Hebrew Alphabet and that every defect in our present world stems from the absence of this letter. When this letter is revealed, then all of the defects will disappear, and it will create new words, new worlds. Finally, all will be complete. A Talmudic legend tells that this 23rd letter appeared on the original set of tablets upon which the ten commandments were inscribed. When the tablets were broken, all letters flew off the tablets and ascended to Heaven. The other letters eventually returned but the 23rd letter had vanished from this world. When this missing letter appears, the world will be balanced once again. This missing letter also signifies the sound beyond all sounds. It represents the last word, the word beyond all words. When the Letter of the Mothers, lost for so long, combines with all of the others letters, it will create a universe of harmony and peace. This is the Messianic Age and will be marked by the harmonious blending of the masculine and the feminine. Then, the Skekhinah, the feminine aspect of the Divine, will be united with the masculine and a new Eden will flourish.*

As quoted in (The Oracle of Kabbalah), when choosing this letter perhaps the best response is to just be quiet. I find this very interesting because when this energy is in motion, this is what you hear, the *Quiet.* This energy *is beyond space, beyond time in the Presence of God.*

According to (The Oracle of Kabbalah), where this information was found and quoted from, *this age will be the Messianic age.* Sean Davis Morton, who is a former renowned remote viewer, for the government, also called this age, *The Messianic Age,* in one of his newsletters, Delphi. Adolphina has been given this letter/symbol for YATUVAY in the representation of this very timeframe, this age. The Talmudic legend says that *when the 23rd letter of the Hebrew Alphabet came into being, that the world could be healed and all defects will disappear.*

I will give you a few case histories to show you the power of Energy Medicine through YATUVAY, formerly called Ascension Healing. Names have been changed for the privacy and protection of the client.

- Paula was an extremely overweight woman in her fifties when she first came to me. Paula had many challenges. When she first came to me, she brought a full-page list of about twenty-eight diagnosed ailments. She said I was her last hope, having exhausted all other medical options. She could not walk more than a half of a block without being winded. She was a diabetic and her endocrine system was not working at all. She had human growth hormone levels of zero. She had to take human growth hormone to sustain life. She was diagnosed with Chronic Fatigue Syndrome and Fibromyalgia. She had polyps lining her throat, esophagus and colon. After a six-month period of bi-monthly sessions, she was no longer diabetic and she was weaning off human growth hormone, as her own levels were rising. The Chronic Fatigue, Fibromyalgia and polyps were gone and she was losing weight. All of these miracles were a result of repairing the Electromagnetic Body.

• Mary was an elderly woman in her seventies. Mary had many challenges. She had heart challenges and could not walk more than a quarter of a block without being winded. She was diabetic. She had a huge purple bump on her back, the size and color of a purple plum, which no one had been able to resolve. She, too, after a six-month period of bi-monthly sessions, was in much better health. Her heart challenges were not nearly as severe. She was no longer winded. Her insulin was down to almost nothing. Mary's blood pressure had stabilized. The purple plum was completely gone. When we ended our sessions last year, Mary told me in tears, *Thank you so much for your help. I know it was you that brought me back to life. I could never repay you for all that you have done.*

• Justin had a very long history of learning disabilities since childhood. He was labeled Dyslexic, ADHD, Bi-Polar and Asthmatic. He had high blood pressure, stomach problems, and high cholesterol, and was on medication for all of the above. Justin was too mentally unstable to work, and needed a nap every day. Within a few months of sessions, his ADHD was under control. With Blueprint Restoration, the Bi-Polar challenge was no longer evident. He no longer needed his asthma medicine. He has been able to wean off some medications and reads as quickly as you read or I do today.

• David was a man in his seventies who was in poor health and had edema. He was an Asthmatic and felt as if his vitality, health and life were slipping away. When he spoke, his voice was very weak and tremulous. He called me *his pow wow doctor* because, when he was a young boy, his grandmother took him to see an Indian Medicine Woman for any ailments, and that is what they called her. After just four sessions, David could breathe much better. His edema was gone. His body and voice were restored and he felt stronger and healthier. Such is the power of YATUVAY.

• Ralph was guided to see me after meeting me at a Mind, Body and Spirit Expo. All of his life, he suffered psychotic episodes, where he acted inappropriately. He heard voices telling him to do things that were against his nature, but he was helpless not to. Eventually, we did get to the root of the problem, which was something that most people are completely unaware can exist. In another lifetime, Ralph had practiced Black Magic, where he harmed many people with his magical knowledge and skills. What eventually came to light is that when you practice Black Magic, you receive a demon seed, which grows in strength over time. Even if you pray for the dark side, this can occur. *Never pray for the dark side, as this is very dangerous for you!* Through reincarnation, this demon became a part of his very Souls' blueprint. This is what can be called *very bad, bad karma,* because karma is a balanced scale, where you reap what you have sowed. Alternatively, to look at this subject another way, as the consequence for his actions. It took several years for Ralph to start feeling better, as it was necessary to get rid of something that was part of his very cellular structure. It was not an easy process for Ralph, but today he is somewhat better, with no psychotic episodes.

There are some Light workers or Energy Medicine Practitioners, who utilize universal energy, but who may be unable to perform some of the above listed techniques *unless they change their energetic methodology or modality to that of YATUVAY.* This is for two reasons. The first is that some Light workers do not have the necessary frequency or vibration, and will need to raise their vibration through the Basic-Seven-Step-Repair-System first. Many may need repeated energetic cleansing, and daily salt baths, to raise their vibration.

This is because their systems have the potential to have been compromised, from the previous energy work that they have done, without knowing how to properly cleanse themselves through Energetic Hygiene. Many most likely will require the Striking Technique, to clear out all of the negative energies that they have absorbed from working on sick people. For an Energy Medicine Practitioner, The Striking Technique needs to be done once or twice a year, for those who practice Energy Medicine regularly.

The other reason is, prior to reading this book; they were not working directly with The Holy Trinity, as Adolphina and her students are. Most Light workers work with Ascended Masters *utilizing universal energy* in their healing work. Universal energy is not the highest energy in the world because it contains within it all of the anger, angst, fear, and pain that humanity has ever experienced. Additionally, there simply are no Ascended Masters, who can touch the reach and power of our Creator. If you want to reach the pinnacle of *The Power Of One*, you must follow these techniques to the letter, and not comprise the quality of the work by integrating other modalities.

You might liken some of the advanced techniques described in this book as requiring 220 volts of electricity, whereas many Energy Medicine Practitioners currently only have a 110 volts boost of electricity. Using this analogy, initiations and at-one-ments given directly by The Holy Trinity, have boosted YATUVAY Practitioners to 220 volts of electricity. If someone has a voltage of 110 volts, and they attempt to run 220 volts through their body, what do you suppose might happen? The answer is the same thing that would happen if you plugged a 110-volt appliance into a 220-volt supply, the appliance would be fried. This same theory applies to the frequency of an Energy Medicine Practitioner. This is why for those of you who cannot yet partake of the YATUVAY frequencies, until they raise their own frequency through the Basic-Seven-Step-Repair-System, that the energy will automatically be adjusted to *Adolphina Shephards' Ascension Healing* frequencies and vibration.

Healers can only channel up to the frequency to which they are attuned. This is just plain common sense.

However, all have the potential to channel this energy, by upgrading your frequency, and by developing communication with our Creator. Otherwise, as previously mentioned, the energy will be automatically diverted, to the former modality of Ascension Healings frequencies and vibrations. This is the next most potent energy that works with, The Lord Jesus Christ, and his Universes. In time, as the strength of your Spiritual Bodies grows, there is far greater potential for being able to channel the YATUVAY frequencies. This is because your energetic muscles work the same way as muscles work in the Physical Body. *The muscle strengthens as you use that muscle.* However, it does require *one more thing and that is faith.* Do you remember a saying from the Bible that goes something like this, *you can move a mountain with faith the size of a mustard seed?* For your information, I use the New American Standard Edition of the Bible although I have various other Bible versions as well.

In answering this chapter's question, what do we do now? I strongly suggest finding a way to de-stress, whether you take up yoga, qigong, tai chi, long walks, music or reading. Do whatever it takes to de-stress because stress is the major reason for many illnesses that occur and then fester.

You must take control of your thought processes. This is vital! You must watch the words that come out of your mouth, because your words contain the power of life or death. Additionally, I suggest that you adopt a more natural way of eating, by not eating many processed foods, and eating more vegetables, salads, and fruits. For total wellness, you must get some exercise. Our bodies were not designed to sit in front of computers all day long and televisions all night long. They were built to move. Stagnant energy in a body creates stagnant fluids, thus creating total body stagnation, which creates illness. Get those bodies moving! Take a bike ride. Climb the stairs instead of taking the elevator. Take a long walk. Exercise doesn't need to be complicated.

I also recommend that you take up meditation and prayer in order to reconnect with The Holy Trinity, as most of us have fallen away from direct contact. *Prayer is when you talk to God and meditation is when you listen to God.* I believe that this falling away from direct contact has occurred because for so many centuries, people have been lead to believe that they needed a priest, pastor, minister, reverend, rabbi or some type of intercessor to communicate with The Holy Trinity. Nothing could be further from the truth, as The Lord, would like us all to be in communion with him. We have been educated by organized religions to believe that we need an intercessor between God, and ourselves. This is a grave disservice to humanity and results in our disconnecting from the very Source that gives us life.

However, perhaps we were not evolved enough for this in past generations. What organized religion gave us was a moral compass by which to live that was necessary in order for the human race to evolve. Now, however, many people are spiritually ready to take the next step, to evolve to the level of direct contact with our Creator. Father is highly desirous for this to occur.

Furthermore, I suggest that you consider taking some classes in Energy Medicine in order to stay healthy. Alternatively, have a maintenance schedule by which to maintain your health. Most people have a regular schedule of maintenance for their looks, such as a monthly haircut or color, a weekly manicure and/or massage. Perhaps even, work out at a gym daily. Most people regularly see a dentist to keep their teeth in working order and looking good too. If you want to feel as good as you look, doesn't it make sense to keep the whole you in good shape?

There are many different modalities of Energy Medicine that exist, but the only one I can vouch for is YATUVAY, which is the Energy of GOD, previously called Ascension Healing with Adolphina Shephard. I mentioned previously that most Light workers use Universal Energy in their healing sessions, but Universal Energy and the Energy of GOD are two entirely different things. At one time, all energy on Earth was of God, but as the world evolved, everything developed its own frequency and vibration. Hence, that which is called, Universal Energy, taps into the collective energy of the world. With all of the poverty, fear, anger, angst and wars going on in our collective world, this energy is not of the very highest vibration, as is The Energy Medicine of YATUVAY.

Utilizing Universal Energy is part of the reason why we do not hear about many miraculous healings through Energy Medicine. However, our Creator can and will create miraculous healings, when we are directly communicating and participating with our Creator. God has all of the power of the universe in his hands. It is up to us to ask and we shall receive. There are several different ways to receive these miraculous healing sessions.

- The first is to schedule a private consultation with a YATUVAY Practitioner. Usually, there is no instant fix but rather a couple of months of one or two sessions a month. Other times, it may take a little longer depending on the problem.

- The second recommendation is to take Energy Medicine classes through YATUVAY. This enables you to learn to heal yourself and your loved ones.

- Third recommendation is that you can become an Energy Medicine Practitioner yourself, by taking Energy Medicine Classes. This will enable you to heal yourself, heal your loved ones and, *assist with healing others.*

- However, before this can occur, you must undergo personal healing of self, in order to receive the vibration from The Holy Trinity in order to assist others. This healing will take place as you use the Basic-Seven-Step-Repair-System. The seventh step, Striking, will need to be done either by an experienced practitioner of YATUVAY, or by taking a class, where you will learn how to do this.

There are many Advanced Energy Medicine Practitioners, who have worked very hard to heal themselves and do wonderful work. These energy practitioners will have no problem utilizing the YATUVAY methods. For these Energy Medicine Practitioners, the reference material in Chapter 7 will be very welcome, as it will present them with a total picture of how to create wellness for many people.

I suspect that, eventually, there will be a major switch in the medical field, in which we will no longer treat just the symptoms or cut out the tumor, but also get to the root of the problem, through the Spiritual Bodies, by utilizing Energy Medicine, diet and exercise. This is not said to dismiss the medical field, as it stands, because many lives have been saved by having that surgery or taking that pill. Rather, Energy

Medicine is used as preventative care. Energy Medicine is also used curatively, where many miraculous healings will occur. We should use Energy Medicine in conjunction with traditional medicine, in order to bring a person back to total wellness, as the physical body needs to be supported while the curative energy assimilates into the body.

There are bi-monthly *Circles of Healing*, where YATUVAY Practitioners work on each other in order to keep their own Electromagnetic Bodies in tiptop shape. Clinics are held once a month, in which we assist those who cannot afford to pay for their sessions. Should you decide to become a practitioner of this modality, you can attend The Circle of Healing, or form your own local Circle of Healing. If you are ill and would like to have a private consultation with a YATUVAY Practitioner, please see Adolphina Shephard's website at www.AdolphinaShephard.com, where you will find contact information to reach a YATUVAY Practitioner.

Lastly, we must work on our emotions by recognizing the spiritual cause behind the physical illness. In the next chapter, Chapter 7, you will find an alphabetized list of physical ailments that lists the spiritual cause behind it, and the Energy Medicine Techniques that have the potential to restore a person to wellness through the healing of the Electromagnetic Body.

CHAPTER 7 ~

The Manual

It is my belief that most physical challenges stem from a spiritual issue that exists on the spiritual plane and sub-exists on a subconscious level. This is because all illness starts first on the spiritual level, and then works its way to the mental, the emotional and, finally, as a consequence of the other bodies, the physical level. So, in order to have an illness not reappear once physically resolved, the spiritual, emotional and mental aspects must also be addressed. For this reason, I have included in this chapter the emotion that I believe is responsible for the illness to have taken root. For the most part, I believe that our big emotional downfall is unconscious *FEAR*, in capital letters, which then exhibits itself through anger, sadness and whatever other emotions are experienced.

In this chapter, you will find a list of physical challenges in alphabetical order, along with their probable related cause in the Spiritual, Mental, Emotional and Physical Bodies. In the next column, you will find the Energy Medicine techniques required to heal the Electromagnetic Body for each challenge. Lastly, you will find some practical suggestions for healing the Physical Body. Through personal experience, I have found that there is a minimum Seven-Step-Basic-Repair-System, which is necessary to repair the Base Electromagnetic Body. See Chapter 5 for a description of these repairs and systematic instructions. Additional steps are based on each particular challenge. You must perform each particular technique to finalize the transition from illness to wellness, so that the client can thrive instead of just survive. It is a very good idea, to have the client maintain a routine schedule of monthly or bimonthly sessions to maintain their newfound health.

The Manual also includes emotional balancing techniques to bring the client into total emotional balance to ensure that the challenges will not reoccur. The five emotional balancing tools that are used in YATUVAY are Inner Child, Yin/Yang Balancing, Emotional Balancing & Transmutation, Chemical

Balancing and Blueprint Restoration. These techniques are extremely powerful and work in different areas of the brain, the solar plexus, the ovaries, the testes and the esoteric primal brain, which is located in our abdomen. Chapter 5 contains instructions on how to perform three of these balancing techniques. For more information, see Chapter 5.

The number of times a particular technique should be run, as well as the timeline, is listed under the "Probable Repairs & Techniques column. You will note that total time invested to achieve wellness, on all levels of being, spiritual, mental, emotional and physical is a minimal time investment to regain your health.

You will find the remainder of the techniques listed that will resolve the Electromagnetic Body's challenges, and allow the Physical Body to heal naturally in this chapter. This is possible because the Electromagnetic Body supersedes the Physical Body. The Electromagnetic Body is responsible for feeding the Physical Body the energy to sustain life itself. For many of the challenges, you will see that I recommend a chiropractic adjustment. This is because the spine is the grounding rod through which energy flows. If a nerve or meridian is compressed, this will surely affect the health of the client. I am a big believer in chiropractic care as a compliment to Energy Medicine for it provides a natural holistic cure for many ailments. Now, let's get started with the techniques needed to resolve physical, mental, emotional and spiritual challenges in the Electromagnetic Body.

Problem	Probable Cause	Probable Repairs & Techniques Needed To Resolve the Problem
Abdominal Cramps	Fear	Emotional Balancing Inner Child (3-5x 3 mo apart) Yin/Yang Balancing
	Blocked Sacral Chakra	Chakra Balancing
	Meridian Breaks	Meridian Repair
	Vertebra Misalignment	Chiropractic Adjustment Basic-Seven-Step-Repairs For Complete Wellness
Accidents	Rebellion-Anger	Emotional Balancing Yin/Yang Balancing
	Not Able to Communicate	Inner Child (3-5x 3 mo apart)
	Timed Cookie	Time to Absorb the Lesson Basic-Seven-Step-Repair-System For Complete Wellness Additional repairs are dependent on injuries
Addictions	Self-Hatred	Emotional Balancing
	Needs Love, Forgiveness	Inner Child (3-5x 3 mo apart)
	Compassion	Yin/Yang Balancing

Problem	Probable Cause	Probable Repairs & Techniques Needed To Resolve the Problem
		Forgiveness (10x)
		Compassion (10x)
		Love simultaneous w/each technique
	Outdated Cookies	Cookie & Scan Disc (10-20x 1 mo apart)
	Needs Original Blueprint	Blueprint Restoration
		Chemical Balancing (each session)
		Personalized Addiction Prayer
	Possible Possession	Entity Removal
		Basic-Seven-Step-Repair-System For Complete Wellness
ADHD	Brain Damage	Brain Repair (10x)
	Brain Frequency Imbalance	Brain Balancing (5x)
	Food Intolerances	Eliminate Wheat & Gluten From Diet
	Allergies	Get tested For Allergies (Eat Right For Your Blood Type) by Dr. D'Amato
		Basic-Seven-Step-Repairs For Complete Wellness
Adrenal Problems	Fear/Overwhelmed	Inner Child (3-5x 3 mo apart)
		Emotional Balancing
		Yin/Yang Balancing
	Over-Extension of Abilities	Battery Recharging
	Empty Gas Tank	Prana Tube Filling
	Meridian Breaks	Meridian Repair
	Vertebra Misalignment	Chiropractic Adjustment
	Needs Water Element	Frequent Baths, Pool, Ocean,
	Needs Adrenal Support	Adrenal Support Vitamins
		Chemical Balancing
		Basic-Seven-Step-Repair-System For Complete Wellness
Alcoholism	Hiding Fear	Inner Child (3-5x 3 mo apart)
	Feeling Lost And Inadequate	Emotional Balancing Yin/Yang Balancing
	Possible Possession	Entity Removal
		Forgiveness (10x 1-2x wk)
		Karma Transmutation (20x 1x mo)
		Implantation of New Program
		Personalized Addiction Prayer
		Love Technique w/all Simultaneously
		Chemical Balancing w/all sessions
		Basic-Seven-Step-Repair-System

Problem	Probable Cause	Probable Repairs & Techniques Needed To Resolve the Problem
		For Complete Wellness
Allergies	Something Bothering You	Emotional Balancing
		Yin/Yang Balancing
		Inner Child (3-5x 3 mo apart)
	Meridian Breaks	Meridian Repair
	Lymph Filled w/Toxins	Total Body Lymphatic Cleansing (3x)
	Vertebra Misalignment	Chiropractic Adjustment
	Body Energetically Blocked	Striking I & II
	Blocked Occipital/3rd Eye	Chakra Balancing
	Possible Food Intolerance	(Eat Right For Your Blood Type) by Dr. D'Amato
		Basic-Seven-Step-Repair-System For Complete Wellness
Alzheimer's Disease	Fear/Anger	Forgiveness
		Inner Child (3-5x 3 mo apart)
		Yin/Yang Balancing
		Emotional Balancing
	Acidic System	Alkaline Plant-Based Diet
	Acidic Urine On The Brain	(an alkaline diet is the key)
		Lymphatic Technique (5x)
		Alka-Seltzer 1x daily for a week
	Meridian Breaks	Meridian Repair
	Clogged Arteries in Brain	Cardiac Repair (10-12x)
	Broken Crystals	Crystal Repair
	Crown/ 3rd Eye Blocked	Chakra Balancing
	Pinched Nerves	Chiropractic Adjustment
		Basic-Seven-Step-Repair-System For Complete Wellness
Amenorrhea Menstrual	Prefer Masculine Energy	Yin/Yang Balancing
		Emotional Balancing
		Inner Child (3-5x 3 mo apart)
	Fibroids	Hormonal Balancing with Bio-identical Hormones
	Blueprint Out of Balance	Blueprint Restoration
	Blocked Sacral/Solar Plexus	Chakra Balancing
	Vertebra Misalignment	Chiropractic Adjustment
		Basic-Seven-Step-Repair-System For Complete Wellness
Anemia	Not Enough Love	Inner Child (3-5x 3 mo apart)
	Fear	Emotional Balancing
		Yin/Yang Balancing
		Love simultaneous w/each technique

Problem	Probable Cause	Probable Repairs & Techniques Needed To Resolve the Problem
	Congenital	Karma Transmutation (20x 1 mo apart)
	Lack of Plant Protein	Rice/Beans Consumption
	Cannot Absorb B or Iron through Intestines	B-12 Shots and/or Ferratin
	Possible Light Affliction	Consult Privately
	Lack Intrinsic Factor	Basic-Seven-Step-Repair-System For Complete Wellness
Ankles	Cannot Bear Emotional Weight	Emotional Balancing Yin/Yang Balancing Inner Child (3-5x 3 mo apart)
	Body Energetically Blocked	Striking I & II
	Meridian Breaks	Meridian Repair
	Broken Crystals-Ankles	Crystal Repair
	Blocked Chakras	Chakra Balancing
	Ankles, Knees, Feet	Basic-Seven-Step-Repair-System For Complete Wellness
Anorectal Bleeding	Too Much To Do Resulting In Anger at Life Passing By & Frustrated Over Not Getting Everything Done	Simplification of Life Prioritization of Obligations Realistic Expectations
	Emotional Pressure	Emotional Balancing Yin/Yang Balancing Inner Child (3-5x 3 mo apart)
	Hemorrhoids	Sacral Chiropractic Adjustment
	Blocked Root/Sacral	Chakra Balancing
	Acidic Diet	Alkaline Diet Basic-Seven-Step-Repair-System For Complete Wellness
Anus Itching Bleeding (See above)	Unbalanced Emotions Unwanted Thoughts Mental Arguments	Emotional Balancing Inner Child (3-5x 3 mo apart) Yin/Yang Balancing Love simultaneous w/each technique
	Parasites	Nutritional Remedy for Parasites (Take back control) Basic-Seven-Step-Repair-System For Complete Wellness
Anxiety Attacks Breathing Problems or Hyperventilation	Overwhelming Fear Unbalanced Emotions Unwanted Thoughts Mental Arguments	Emotional Balancing Yin/Yang Balancing Inner Child (3-5x 1 mo apart) Chemical Balancing

Problem	Probable Cause	Probable Repairs & Techniques Needed To Resolve the Problem
		Meditation, Yoga, Tai Chi
		Mimulus Bach Flower (drink bottle)
		Rescue Remedy (daily)
		Cookie & Scan Disc (10-20x 1x mo)
		Basic-Seven-Step-Repair-System
		For Complete Wellness
Appetite Excessive	Feeling the Need For Protection	Inner Child (3-5x 3 mo apart)
		Emotional Balancing
		Yin/Yang Balancing
		Chemical Balancing
		Get Sun-20 Min. Daily
	Possible Light Affliction	Consult Privately
		Basic-Seven-Step-Repair-System
		For Complete Wellness
Loss Of Appetite	Fear	Inner Child (3-5x 3 mo apart)
		Emotional Balancing
		Yin/Yang Balancing
	Gas Tank Empty	Prana Tube Filling
	Broken Grids	Grid Repair
	Depleted Batteries	Battery Recharging
		Basic-Seven-Step-Repair-System
		For Complete Wellness
Arteriosclerosis	Closing the Channels of Joy-Your Blood System	Emotional Balancing
		Yin/Yang Balancing
		Inner Child (3-5x 3 mo apart)
		Love simultaneous w/each technique
	Clogged Arteries	Cardiac Repair (10-15x)
		Red Yeast Rice (500 mg taken at night)
	Simple Carb Diet	Complex Carb, Protein & Plant
		Based Diet
	Acidic Diet	Alkaline Diet Is Key
	Food Intolerances by Dr. D'Amato	(Eat Right For Your Blood Type)
		Basic-Seven-Step-Repair-System
		For Complete Wellness
Arthritis	Fear	Emotional Balancing
		Yin/Yang Balancing
		Inner Child (3-5x 3 mo apart)
	Meridian Breaks	Meridian Repair
	Chakra Blocks	Chakra Balancing
	Vertebra Misalignment	Regular Chiropractic Adjustments
	Bones Fusing Together	Massage with Peanut Oil

Problem	Probable Cause	Probable Repairs & Techniques Needed To Resolve the Problem
		(Weekly)
	Food Intolerance	(Eat Right For Your Blood Type) by Dr. D'Amato
		Starch Elimination
		Eight Glasses of Water With A Little Juice In It (daily)
		Crab Apple Bach Flower Remedy
		Ginger Tea
	Lack of exercise	Tai Chi, Qigong, Yoga, Pilates, Walk Swimming, Physical Therapy
	Karma	Karma Transmutation (10-20x)
	Lack of Forgiveness	Forgiveness (8x 1 wk apart)
	Virus (Ankylosing Spondylitis)	Viral Neutralization (10x) Cellular Release (3x)
	Genetic Factors	DNA Repair - Genetic (5x)
	Broken Crystals	Crystal Repair
	Body Crying For Rest	Take 1-2 days Off Just To Recharge A Week
	Lymph Filled W/Toxins	Total Body Lymphatic Cleansing
		Hot Epsom/Mineral Salt Baths
		Linolenic Acid
		Oleic Acid
		Basic-Seven-Step-Repair-System For Complete Wellness
Asthma	Sadness	Emotional Balancing
	Grief	Yin/Yang Balancing
	Fear of Known Things	Inner Child (3-5x 3 mo apart) Mimulus Bach Flower (drink bottle)
	Broken Meridians	Meridian Repair
	Heart Strangled By Cords	Cord Cutting
	Blocked Heart Chakra	Chakra Balancing
	Body Energetically Blocked	Striking I & II
		Basic-Seven-Step-Repair-System For Complete Wellness
Athlete's Foot	Unbalanced Intestinal Track From Simple Carb, Sugar Diet and/or Antiboitics	Complex Carb, Protein, Veggie Diet (Eat Right For Your Blood Type) by Dr. D'Amato
		Yogurt With Live Cultures daily
		Take Probiotics
		Processed Food Elimination
		Foot Soak w/Epsom Salts
		Anti-fungal Cream
		Basic-Seven-Step-Repair-System

Problem	Probable Cause	Probable Repairs & Techniques Needed To Resolve the Problem
		For Complete Wellness
Autism	Lack of Conductivity In the Brain & Fluids in the Body	Organic Sea Salts in Food Sea Salt Baths (2 cups) weekly Ocean (as often as possible) Daily Multi-Mineral Complex Daily Multi-Vitamins Complex
	Brain Damage	Brain Repair (20x)
	Allergies	Tested For Allergies
	Food Intolerances	(Eat Right For Your Blood Type) by Dr. D'Amato Basic-Seven-Step-Repair-System For Complete Wellness
Back Problems Lower	Fear	Emotional Balancing Inner Child (3-5x 3 mo apart) Yin/Yang Balancing
	Blocked Sacral Chakra	Chakra Balancing
	Meridian Breaks	Meridian Repair
	Broken Crystals (Spine)	Crystal Repair
	Spinal Damage	Spinal Cord Repair Technique
	Vertebra Misalignment	Chiropractic Adjustment Basic-Seven-Step-Repair-System For Complete Wellness
Middle	Guilt	Inner Child (3-5x 3 mo apart) Karma Transmutation (20x 1 mo apart) Emotional Balancing Yin/Yang Balancing
	Implants	Cookie & Scan Disc Basic-Seven-Step-Repair-System For Complete Wellness
Upper	Weight of World on Shoulders	Inner Child (3-5x 3 mo apart) Yin/Yang Balancing
	Need Support	Emotional Balancing Water Violet Bach Flower Remedy Yin/Yang Balancing
	Implants	Cookie & Scan Disc Basic-Seven-Step-Repair-System For Complete Wellness
Bad Breath	Anger	Inner Child (3-5x 3 mo apart) Emotional Balancing Yin/Yang Balancing

Problem	Probable Cause	Probable Repairs & Techniques Needed To Resolve the Problem
		Forgiveness
		Basic-Seven-Step-Repair-System For Complete Wellness
Baldness	Fear	Inner Child (3-5x 3 mo apart)
		Emotional Balancing
		Yin/Yang Balancing
	Congenital	Karma Transmutation (20x 1 mo apart)
		Basic-Seven-Step-Repair-System For Complete Wellness
Bedwetting	Fear	Emotional Balancing
		Yin/Yang Balancing
		Inner Child (3-5x 3 mo apart)
		Love simultaneous w/each technique
		Basic-Seven-Step-Repair-System For Complete Wellness
Belching	Fear	Inner Child (3-5x 3 mo apart)
		Emotional Balancing
		Yin/Yang Balancing
	Food Intolerance	(Eat Right For Your Blood Type) by Dr. D'Amato
		Basic-Seven-Step-Repair-System For Complete Wellness
Bell's Palsy	Anger Rooted in Fear	Inner Child (3-5x 3 mo apart)
		Emotional Balancing
		Yin/Yang Balancing
		Basic-Seven-Step-Repair-System For Complete Wellness
Birth Defects	Karma-Unfinished Business from Prior Lives	Karma Transmutation (20x 1 mo apart)
		Emotional Balancing
		Inner Child (3-5x 3 mo apart)
		Yin/Yang Balancing
		Basic-Seven-Step-Repair-System For Complete Wellness
Bladder Problems	Fear/Anxiety	Karma Transmutation (20x 1 mo apart)
		Emotional Balancing
		Inner Child (3-5x 3 mo apart)
		Yin/Yang Balancing
	Broken Meridians	Meridian Repair
	Leaking Urine	Kegel Exercises Daily
	Nerve/Spine Damage	Spinal Repair (3x)

Problem	Probable Cause	Probable Repairs & Techniques Needed To Resolve the Problem
		Basic-Seven-Step-Repair-System For Complete Wellness
Blood Problems (Ex. Leukemia, Anemia)	Lack of Love	Love (10x as needed) Emotional Balancing Inner Child (3-5x 3 mo apart) Yin/Yang Balancing
	Blood Defect Lack of Intrinsic Factor Lack of Plant Protein	B-12 Shots (weekly, then monthly) Rice/Beans Consumption Basic-Seven-Step-Repair-System For Complete Wellness
Blood Pressure High (Hypertension)	Emotional Challenge	Emotional Balancing Inner Child (3-5x 3 mo apart) Yin/Yang Balancing
	Clogged Arteries	Cardiac Repair (10-12x) Red Yeast Rice (500 mg at bedtime)
	Unbalanced Chemistry Lack of Sunlight Use of Nasal Spray or Decongestants Lack of Exercise Simple Carb, Sugar Diet Too Much Protein Acidic Diet	Chemical Balancing (as needed) Daily Sun & Vitamin D Cessation of Nasal Spray & Decongestants Walk, Bike, Tai Chi, Yoga, Pilates Complex Carb, Protein, Veggie, Fruit Diet Alkaline Diet Is Key Celery (4 Stalks Daily) Eight Glasses of Water (Daily) Basic-Seven-Step-Repair-System For Complete Wellness
Low	Lack of Love	Emotional Balancing Inner Child (3-5x 3 mo apart) Yin/Yang Balancing Love simultaneous w/each technique
	Underactive Thyroid	Thyroid Repair & Thyroid Medicine Basic-Seven-Step-Repair-System For Complete Wellness
Body Odor	Fear	Emotional Balancing Inner Child (3-5x 3 mo apart) Yin/Yang Balancing Basic-Seven-Step-Repair-System For Complete Wellness

Problem	Probable Cause	Probable Repairs & Techniques Needed To Resolve the Problem
Boils	Anger	Emotional Balancing Inner Child (3-5x 3 mo apart) Yin/Yang Balancing Love simultaneous w/each technique Basic-Seven-Step-Repair-System For Complete Wellness
Bones (See Blood)	Bone Weakness From Acidic Diet Fear	Yin/Yang Balancing Emotional Balancing Inner Child (3-5x 3 mo apart) Love simultaneous w/each technique
	Acidic Diet	Alkaline Diet Is Key
	Poor Nourishment	Balanced Diet
	Simple Carb, Sugar Diet	Complex Carb, Protein, Veggie, Fruit Diet
	Clogged Veins	Cardiac Repair (10-12x) Weight Bearing Exercise

	Lack of Calcium & D	Calcium & Vitamin D Supplementation
		Calcium Nourishment from Food
		Mimulus & Sweet Chestnut Bach
		  Flower Remedies
		Basic-Seven-Step-Repair-System
		  For Complete Wellness

Bone Deformity
Dowagers Hump
(See above)
	Lack of Forgiveness
	Emotional/Mental Rigidity
		Forgiveness (10-20x)
		Emotional Balancing
		Yin/Yang Balancing
		Inner Child (3-5x 3 mo apart)
		Peanut Oil Massage to Break Down
		  Calcification of Shell Formation
		  (Bi-monthly)
		Trigger Point Injections for Pain

	Broken Crystals Acidic Diet	Crystal Repair Alkaline Plant Based Diet Rehabilitative Exercises for Stretching & Posture
	Injury to the Spine	Spinal Repair (10x) Chiropractic Adjustment Basic-Seven-Step-Repair-System For Complete Wellness
Bowels	Fear	Emotional Balancing Inner Child (3-5x 3 mo apart) Yin/Yang Balancing
	Broken Meridians Cords Strangling Intestines	Meridian Repair Cord Cutting

Problem	Probable Cause	Probable Repairs & Techniques Needed To Resolve the Problem
	Blocked Sacral/Root Chakra	Chakra Balancing
	Not Enough Fiber in Diet	Fruits & Vegetables
	Not Enough Water	Eight Glasses of Water (Daily)
	Lack of Exercise	Walk, Bike, TaiChi, Qigong
	Food Intolerance	(Eat Right For Your Blood Type) by Dr. D'Amato
		Eliminate Wheat & Dairy Products
		Basic-Seven-Step-Repair-System For Complete Wellness
Brain Challenges	Stuck Thoughts (Move them forward with these techniques)	Inner Child (3-5x 3 mo apart) Emotional Balancing Yin/Yang Balancing
	Acidic Diet	Plant-Based Diet
	Poor Nourishment	Balanced Diet
	Simple Carb, Sugar Diet	Complex Carb, Protein, Veggie, Fruit Diet
	Possible Tumor (Latent Tissue Acidosis)	See Specialist
	Toxic Lymphatic System	Lymphatic Technique (5x) Cookie & Scan Disc (10-20x 1 mo)
	Broken Meridians	Meridian Repair
	Broken Grids	Grid Repair
	Blocked Crown Chakra	Chakra Balancing
	Unbalanced Crown Chakra	Grid Repair Karma Transmutation (10-20x)
	Clogged Arteries	Cardiac Repair (10-12x)
	Lack of Exercise	Walk, Bike, Qigong, Tai Chi
	Broken Grids	Grid Repair (5-10x) Medication Side Effects Drug Discontinuance (if permitted), Holistic Approach
	Possible Entity Possession	Entity Removal Basic-Seven-Step-Repair-System For Complete Wellness
Brain Tumor	See above	
	Chronic Cell Phone Use	Cell Phone Use Reduction
	Broken Grids	Grid Repair Esoteric Surgery to Remove Tumor
	Broken Meridians	Meridian Repair
	Blocked Chakras	Chakra Balancing
	Parasites	Holistic Parasite Remedy Basic-Seven-Step-Repair-System For Complete Wellness

Problem	Probable Cause	Probable Repairs & Techniques Needed To Resolve the Problem
Breath - Loss of See Heart	Out of Balance	Emotional Balancing Yin/Yang Balancing Inner Child (3-5x 3 mo apart) Karma Transmutation (10-20x 1 mo) Basic-Seven-Step-Repair-System For Complete Wellness
Bronchitis	Grief/Sadness	Emotional Balancing Inner Child (3-5x 3 mo apart) Yin/Yang Balancing Health Program
	Lack of Forgiveness Cords Strangling Heart Viral/Bacterial Infection Toxic Lymphatic System	Forgiveness (5-10x) Cord Cutting Viral/Bacterial Neutralization Lymphatic Technique (5x) Cellular Release

	Outdated Programs
	Low Immune System
		Cookie & Scan Disc (10x 1 mo apart)
		Rest, Good Nutrition, Exercise, Sun, Fun
		Positive Affirmations such as
		  "I Am Healthy, Happy & Terrific"
		Basic-Seven-Step-Repair-System
		  For Complete Wellness

Bulimia	Fear of Known Things	Emotional Balancing Inner Child (3-5x 3 mo apart) Yin/Yang Balancing Mimulus Bach Flower Remedy Basic-Seven-Step-Repair-System For Complete Wellness

Cancer	Negative Self-Talk
	Fear Of Known Things
	Low Self-Esteem
	Latent Tissue Acidosis
	  Or Acidic Diet
		Healing Assessment - Is It Person's
		  Path to be Cured?
		
		The KEY-Alkaline Plant Based Diet
		  Alka-Seltzer daily for a week
		  Juicing of Fresh Vegetables & Fruit

	Viral Infection	Viral Neutralization Cellular Release Love simultaneous w/each technique Super Greens Organic Raw Foods Diet Tai Chi, Qigong Chinese Herbs - Panax Ginseng Root Positive Affirmations Funny Movies

Problem	Probable Cause	Probable Repairs & Techniques Needed To Resolve the Problem
		Support Group
		Basic-Seven-Step-Repair-System
		For Complete Wellness
Cataracts	Fear of Death	Emotional Balancing
		Inner Child (3-5x 3 mo apart)
		Yin/Yang Balancing
	Broken Meridians	Meridian Repair
	Broken Grids	Grid Repair
	Blocked Eye Chakras	Chakra Balancing
		Basic-Seven-Step-Repair-System
		For Complete Wellness
Canker Sores	Fear	Emotional Balancing
		Inner Child (3-5x 3 mo apart)
		Yin/Yang Balancing
	Acidic Diet	Alkaline Diet
		Lysine (500mg Daily)
		Vitamin C (500mg Daily)
		Basic-Seven-Step-Repair-System
		For Complete Wellness
Cholesterol	Fear of Joy	Emotional Balancing
See Heart		Inner Child (3-5x 3 mo apart)
		Yin/Yang Balancing
	Acidic Diet	Key is Alkaline Diet
	Simple Carb, Sugar Diet	Complex Carb, Protein, Veggie, Fruit
		Diet
		(Eat Right For Your Blood Type)
		by Dr. D'Amato
	Clogged Arteries	Cardiac Repair (10-12x)
		Red Yeast Rice
		Basic-Seven-Step-Repair-System
		For Complete Wellness
Crohn's Disease	See Psoriasis/Arthritis	
Colon Polyps	Fear	Emotional Balancing
		Yin/Yang Balancing
		Inner Child (3-5x 3 mo apart)
	Food Intolerance	(Eat Right For Your Blood Type)
		by Dr. D'Amato
		Eliminate Wheat Products
	Meridian Breaks	Repair Meridians
	Vertebra Misalignment	Chiropractic Adjustment
		Colonoscopy

Problem	Probable Cause	Probable Repairs & Techniques Needed To Resolve the Problem
		Basic-Seven-Step-Repair-System For Complete Wellness
Coma	Fear/Despair	Inner Child (3-5x 3 mo apart) Emotional Balancing Yin/Yang Balancing
	Grid Breaks	Grid Repair
	Meridian Breaks	Meridian Repair
	Broken Crystals	Crystal Repair
	Blocked Chakras	Chakra Balancing Health Program (3-5x) Basic-Seven-Step-Repair-System For Complete Wellness
Crying	Emotional Imbalance	Emotional Balancing Inner Child (3-5x 3 mo apart) Yin/Yang Balancing Bach Flower Rescue Remedy Basic-Seven-Step-Repair-System For Complete Wellness
Cushing's Disease (See Adrenal)	Emotional Imbalance	Emotional Balancing Inner Child (3-5x 3 mo apart) Yin/Yang Balancing Bach Flower Rescue Remedy Basic-Seven-Step-Repair-System For Complete Wellness
Deafness	Emotional Imbalance (What don't you want to Hear?)	Emotional Balancing Inner Child (3-5x 3 mo apart) Yin/Yang Balancing
	Broken Meridians	Meridian Repair
	Chronic Cell Phone Use	Eliminate Cell Phone Use Homeopathic Remedy, *Radiation*
	Wax	Ear Candling
	Ear Infection	Antibiotics
	Vertebrae Misalignment	Chiropractic Adjustment
	Karma	Karma Transmutation (10-20x 1 mo) Basic-Seven-Step-Repair-System For Complete Wellness
Depression	Fear Resulting In Anger Turned Inward	Emotional Balancing Yin/Yang Balancing
	Emotional Imbalance	Inner Child (3-5x 3 mo apart)
	Outdated Programming	Cookie & Scan Disc (10-20x 1 mo)

Problem	Probable Cause	Probable Repairs & Techniques Needed To Resolve the Problem
	Blueprint Imbalance	Blueprint Restoration (3x)
	Lack of Sunlight	20 Minutes Sunshine Daily
	Resulting in Chemical	Vitamin D Supplementation
	Imbalance	Chemical Balancing
		Basic-Seven-Step-Repair-System
		For Complete Wellness
Diabetes	Emotional Imbalance	Emotional Balancing
	(Feeling of "Is that all	
	there is?")	Inner Child (3-5x 3 mo apart)
		Yin/Yang Balancing
	Mental Anguish	Sweet Chestnut Bach Flower Remedy
	Meridian Breaks	Meridian Repair
	High Carbohydrate Diet	High Protein, Veggie, Fruit Diet
	Lack of Exercise	Qigong, Tai Chi, Walk, Bike
		Basic-Seven-Step-Repair-System
		For Complete Wellness
Diarrhea	Fear/Nerves	Emotional Balancing
		Inner Child (3-5x 3 mo apart)
		Yin/Yang Balancing
	Broken Meridians	Meridian Repair
	Blocked Sacral/Root Chakra	Chakra Balancing
	Food Poisoning	Natural Processing of Poison
	Virus	Rest, Water, Nourishment
		Basic-Seven-Step-Repair-System
		For Complete Wellness
Dizziness	Emotional Imbalance	Emotional Balancing
(Vertigo)	Unhappy	Inner Child (3-5x 3 mo apart)
See Heart	Apathy	Yin/Yang Balancing
	Blocked Crown/3rd Eye	Chakra Balancing
	Soul Splitting (crisis)	Soul Retrieval (10-20x 1 mo apart)
	Inner Ear Infection	See Specialist
		Ginkgo Biloba
	Wax in Ear	Ear Candling
	Total Exhaustion	Rest
	Dehydration	Fluids
		Basic-Seven-Step-Repair-System
		For Complete Wellness
Edema	What Are You Holding	Emotional Balancing
See Heart	Onto Past Its Time?	Yin/Yang Balancing
		Inner Child (3-5x 3 mo apart)
	Cords Strangling Heart	Cord Cutting
	Broken Meridians	Meridian Repair

Problem	Probable Cause	Probable Repairs & Techniques Needed To Resolve the Problem
	Broken Grids	Grid Repair
	Blocked Chakras	Chakra Balancing
	Body Energetically Blocked	Striking I & II
	Toxic Lymphatic System	Lymphatic Technique (5x)
		Basic-Seven-Step-Repair-System For Complete Wellness
Elbows	Difficulty w/Changes in Life	Emotional Balancing
		Yin/Yang Balancing
		Inner Child (3-5x 3 mo apart)
	Broken Crystals	Crystal Repair
		Basic-Seven-Step-Repair-System For Complete Wellness
Emphysema	Fear/Grief	Emotional Balancing
	Over Concern for	Inner Child (3-5x 3 mo apart)
	Loved Ones	Yin/Yang Balancing
	Living in the Past	Cookie & Scan Disc (10-20x 1 mo)
	Broken Grids	Grid Repair (3-5x)
	Blocked Heart/Chakra	Chakra Balancing
	Extreme Exhaustion	Battery Recharging
		Rest
	Empty Gas Tank	Prana Tube Filling
	Body Energetically Blocked	Striking I & II
	Cords Strangling Heart	Cord Cutting
	Broken Lung/Heart Meridian	Meridian Repair
	Cigarette Smoking	Smoking Cessation
		Basic-Seven-Step-Repair-System For Complete Wellness
Epilepsy	Mentally/Emotionally Escaping Life's Challenges	Emotional Balancing
		Yin/Yang Balancing
	Overwhelmed by Responsibility	Inner Child (3-5x 3 mo apart)
		Elm Bach Flower Remedy
	Broken Grids Disrupting Electrical Signals in Brain	Grid Repair w/all
	Broken Meridians (GV, CV, Possibly Gallbladder)	Meridian Repair
	Broken Crystals	Crystal Repair
	Devices	Device Removal
	Electromagnetic Wounds	Wound Sealing
		Health Program as needed
		Basic-Seven-Step-Repair-System For Complete Wellness
Epstein-Barr Virus	Fear Of Not Living Up To	Emotional Balancing

Problem	Probable Cause	Probable Repairs & Techniques Needed To Resolve the Problem
	Standards of Others	Inner Child (3-5x 3 mo apart)
	Unwanted Mental Thoughts	Yin/Yang Balancing
	& Arguments	White Chestnut Bach Flower Remedy
	Holes in Grids	Grid Repair
	Broken Meridians	Meridian Repair
	Overextension	Battery Recharging
	Need Water Element	Regular Baths w/2 cups Mineral Salt
	Empty Gas Tank	Prana Tube Filling
	Underlying Virus	Viral Transmutation (5x)
		Cellular Release (5x)
	Toxic Lymphatic System	Lymphatic Technique (5x)
		Karma Transmutation (10-20x 1 mo)
		Lysine (500 mg daily)
		Basic-Seven-Step-Repair-System For Complete Wellness
Eye Problems	Fear	Emotional Balancing
	What do you not want to see?	Yin/Yang Balancing
		Inner Child (3-5x 3 mo apart)
	Meridian Breaks	Meridian Repair
	Cholesterol Blockage Preventing Blood Flow	Cardiac Repair (10-12x)
	Blocked Eye Chakras	Eye Chakra Balancing
		Basic-Seven-Step-Repair-System For Complete Wellness
Children	Fear of Seeing	Emotional Balancing
		Inner Child (3-5x 3 mo apart)
		Yin/Yang Balancing
		Basic-Seven-Step-Repair-System For Complete Wellness
Glaucoma	Unforgiving	Forgiveness (10x)
	Feeling Overwhelmed by Responsibility	Emotional Balancing
		Inner Child (3-5x 3 mo apart)
		Yin/Yang Balancing
		Basic-Seven-Step-Repair-System For Complete Wellness
Far-sighted	Fear	Emotional Balancing
	Living in the past	Inner Child (3-5x 3 mo apart)
		Yin/Yang Balancing
		Basic-Seven-Step-Repair-System For Complete Wellness
Near-sighted	Fear	Emotional Balancing

Problem	Probable Cause	Probable Repairs & Techniques Needed To Resolve the Problem
	Living in the past	Inner Child (3-5x 3 mo apart) Yin/Yang Balancing Basic-Seven-Step-Repair-System For Complete Wellness
Fat Overweight	Fear Protection from Change & Unwanted Influences Lack of Confidence	Emotional Balancing Inner Child (3-5x 3 mo apart) Yin/Yang Balancing Basic-Seven-Step-Repair-System For Complete Wellness
Fatigue	Depression	Emotional Balancing Yin/Yang Balancing Inner Child (3-5x 3 mo apart)
	Holes in Aura	Grid Repair
	Broken Meridians	Meridian Repair
	Empty Gas Tank	Prana Tube Filling
	Batteries Need Charging	Battery Recharging
	Emotional/Mental Reserves Empty	Recharge The Reserves
	Need Water Element	Tub, Ocean, Pool, etc. Basic-Seven-Step-Repair-System For Complete Wellness
Female Problems	Stuck In the Past (possible prior lives)	Cookie & Scan Disc (5x close timeframe, then 5x 1 mo apart)
	Yin/Yang out of balance (female/male balance)	Yin/Yang Balancing Emotional Balancing Inner Child (3-5x 3 mo apart)
	Hormonal Imbalance	Bio-Identical Hormones Basic-Seven-Step-Repair-System For Complete Wellness
Fever	Anger	Emotional Balancing Yin/Yang Balancing Inner Child (3-5x 3 mo apart) Health Program
	Acidic Body	Alkaline Diet Alka-Seltzer (3 days)
	Weakened Immune System	Live Foods Chicken Soup Tai Chi, Qigong, Yoga Bike, Walk, Nature
	Food Intolerance	(Eat Right For Your Blood Type) by Dr. D'Amato Basic-Seven-Step-Repair-System

Problem	Probable Cause	Probable Repairs & Techniques Needed To Resolve the Problem
		For Complete Wellness
Fibroid Tumors & Cysts	Emotional Pain	Emotional Balancing Yin/Yang Balancing Inner Child (3-5x 3 mo apart)
	Possible Hormonal Imbalance	Bio-Identical Hormones
	Acidic Diet	Alkaline Diet Basic-Seven-Step-Repair-System For Complete Wellness
Fingers (see arthritis)	Meridian Breaks	Meridian Repair
	Blocked Finger/Hand Chakras	Chakra Balancing
	Broken Crystals	Crystal Repair
	Nerve Damage	EMG-Nerve Repair
	Spinal Stenosis	MRI-Spinal Repair Basic-Seven-Step-Repair-System For Complete Wellness
Thumb	Lungs and Grief Represents God	Emotional Balancing Yin/Yang Balancing Inner Child (3-5x 3 mo apart) Prayer & Meditation on God
	Meridian Breaks	Meridian Repair
	Blocked Finger/Hand Chakras	Chakra Balancing
	Broken Crystals	Crystal Repair
	Nerve Damage	EMG-Nerve Repair
	Spinal Stenosis	MRI-Spinal Repair
	Body Energetically Blocked	Basic-Seven-Step-Repair-System For Complete Wellness
Index Finger	Fear	Emotional Balancing Yin/Yang Balancing Inner Child (3-5x 3 mo apart)
	Meridian Block/Break	Meridian Repair
	Blocked Finger/Hand Chakras	Chakra Balancing
	Broken Crystals	Crystal Repair
	Nerve Damage	EMG-Nerve Repair
	Spinal Stenosis	MRI-Spinal Repair Basic-Seven-Step-Repair-System For Complete Wellness
Middle Finger	Anger, Sexual Issues	Emotional Balancing

Problem	Probable Cause	Probable Repairs & Techniques Needed To Resolve the Problem
	Heart (Pericardium) Issues	Yin/Yang Balancing
		Inner Child (3-5x 3 mo apart)
		Cardiac Repair (10-12x)
		See Heart Doctor
	Meridian Block/Break	Meridian Repair
	Blocked Finger/Hand Chakras	Chakra Balancing
	Broken Crystals	Crystal Repair
	Nerve Damage	EMG-Nerve Repair
	Spinal Stenosis	MRI-Spinal Repair
		Basic-Seven-Step-Repair-System For Complete Wellness
Ring Finger	What's Bothering Your Heart Emotionally?	Emotional Balancing
		Yin/Yang Balancing
		Inner Child (3-5x 3 mo apart)
	Represents Triple Warmer (Heart Issues)	Cardiac Repair (10-12x)
		See Heart Doctor
	Meridian Breaks	Meridian Repair
	Blocked Finger/Hand Chakras	Chakra Balancing
	Broken Crystals	Crystal Repair
	Nerve Damage	EMG-Nerve Repair
	Spinal Stenosis	MRI-Spinal Repair
		Basic-Seven-Step-Repair-System For Complete Wellness
Pinky Finger See heart	What's Bothering Your Heart Emotionally?	Emotional Balancing
	Represents Heart	Yin/Yang Balancing
		Inner Child (3-5x 3 mo apart)
	Potential Heart Challenge	Cardiac Repair (10-12x)
		See Heart Doctor
	Meridian Block/Break	Meridian Repair
	Blocked Finger/Hand Chakras	Chakra Balancing
	Broken Crystals	Crystal Repair
	Nerve Damage	EMG-Nerve Repair
	Spinal Stenosis	MRI-Spinal Repair
		Basic-Seven-Step-Repair-System For Complete Wellness
Fibromylagia	Fear	Emotional Balancing
		Yin/Yang Balancing
		Inner Child (3-5x 3 mo apart)

Problem	Probable Cause	Probable Repairs & Techniques Needed To Resolve the Problem
	Latent Tissue Acidosis	Alkaline Diet Is The Key
	Broken Grids	Grid Repair
	Holes in the Aura	
	Broken Meridians	Meridian Repair
	Body Energetically Blocked	Striking I & II
	Emotional/Mental Reserves	Low Charge Reserves
	Adrenaline Burnout	Battery Recharging Adrenaline Supplement
	Meridians Misfiring	See Acupuncturist
	Pain Due To Rips & Tears In Fascia from It Sticking To Frame Of Body	Myofacial Release (2 x a mo)
	Lack of Human Growth Hormone	Hormone Replacement
	Damage to Pituitary & Pineal Glands	Endocrine Repair
	Nerve Pain, Lack of Sleep	Elavil (lowest dosage at bedtime) Chamomile Tea Laced w/Dried Ginger Power (before bed)
	Food Intolerance	(Eat Right For Your Blood Type) by Dr. D'Amato Live Foods
	Misaligned Vertebrae	Chiropractic Adjustment
	Lack of fresh Air & Exercise	Tai Chi, Qigong, Walk, Bike Basic-Seven-Step-Repair-System For Complete Wellness
Fistula (Hemorrhoids)	Fear	Emotional Balancing
	Tiredness at the Thought Of Doing Something	Need Rest 2 Days A Week Yin/Yang Balancing Inner Child (3-5x 3 mo apart)
	Vertebrae Misalignment	Chiropractic Adjustment
	Blocked Chakras	Chakra Balancing
	Meridian Block/Break	Meridian Repair Basic-Seven-Step-Repair-System For Complete Wellness
Flatulence	Fear, Shock	Emotional Balancing Yin/Yang Balancing Inner Child (3-5x 3 mo apart)
	Vertebrae Misalignment	Chiropractic Adjustment
	Blocked Chakras	Chakra Balancing
	Meridian Block/Break	Meridian Repair
	Food Intolerance	(Eat Right For Your Blood Type) by Dr. D'Amato Basic-Seven-Step-Repair-System

Problem	Probable Cause	Probable Repairs & Techniques Needed To Resolve the Problem
		For Complete Wellness
Flu Influenza	Fear	Emotional Balancing Yin/Yang Balancing Inner Child (3-5x 3 mo apart)
	Vitamin D Deficiency	Vitamin D (1,000 units daily in winter)
	Virus	Viral Neutralization Cellular Release
	Lowered Immune System Exercise	Rest, Sun, Nutritious Food, Water, Basic-Seven-Step-Repair-System For Complete Wellness
Foot Problems	What Is Keeping You from Stepping Forward? Fear Broken Meridians Broken Grids Blocked Feet Chakras Broken Crystals Sciatic Karma	Emotional Balancing Yin/Yang Balancing Inner Child (3-5x 3 mo apart) Meridian Repair Grid Repair Chakra Balancing Crystal Repair Chiro Adjustment Karma Transmutation (3x) Basic-Seven-Step-Repair-System For Complete Wellness
Big Toe	Anger	Yin/Yang Balancing Emotional Balancing Inner Child (3-5x 3 mo apart)
	Represents Spleen Meridian Block/Break Liver/Spleen Blocked Chakras Body Energetically Blocked Vertebrae Misalignment	See Medical Doctor Meridian Repair Chakra Balancing Striking I & II Chiropractic Adjustment Basic-Seven-Step-Repair-System For Complete Wellness
Toe next to Big toe	Meridian Breaks (Stomach) Blocked Chakras Body Energetically Blocked Vertebrae Misalignment	Meridian Repair Chakra Balancing Striking I & II Chiropractic Adjustment Basic-Seven-Step-Repair-System For Complete Wellness
Middle Toe	Inability to Choose	Yin/Yang Balancing

Problem	Probable Cause	Probable Repairs & Techniques Needed To Resolve the Problem
	Between Alternatives	Emotional Balancing
	Meridian Block/Break	Meridian Repair
	Blocked Chakras	Chakra Balancing
	Energetically Blocked	Striking I & II
	Vertebrae Misalignment	Chiropractic Adjustment
		Basic-Seven-Step-Repair-System For Complete Wellness
Toe next to Pinky	Fear Of Knowing Things	Inner Child (3-5x 3 mo apart)
		Yin/Yang Balancing
		Emotional Balancing
	Meridian Breaks	Meridian Repair
	Gallbladder	Gallbladder Repair
	Possible Gallstones	Esoteric Surgery to Remove Stones
	Blocked Chakras	Chakra Balancing
	Body Energetically Blocked	Striking I & II
	Vertebrae Misalignment	Chiropractic Adjustment
		Mimulus Bach Flower (drink bottle)
		Basic-Seven-Step-Repair-System For Complete Wellness
Pinky Toe	Bladder Meridian Block/Break	Meridian Repair
	Blocked Chakras	Chakra Balancing
	Body Energetically Blocked	Striking I & II
	Vertebrae Misalignment	Chiropractic Adjustment
		Basic-Seven-Step-Repair-System For Complete Wellness
Fractures	Hopelessness/Despair	Inner Child (3-5x 3 mo apart)
		Emotional Balancing
		Yin/Yang Balancing
	Lowered Immune System	Rest, Sun, Nutritious Food, Water, Exercise
	Acidic Diet Leaching Calcium from Bones	Calcium Rich Foods & Supplementation
		Alkaline Plant Based Diet
		(Eat Right For Your Blood Type) by Dr. D'Amato
		Basic-Seven-Step-Repair-System For Complete Wellness
Frigidity	Fear	Inner Child (3-5x 3 mo apart)
		Emotional Balancing
		Yin/Yang Balancing
	Blocked Sacral/Root Chakra	Chakra Balancing
	Meridian Breaks	Meridian Repair

Problem	Probable Cause	Probable Repairs & Techniques Needed To Resolve the Problem
	Hormonal Imbalance	Hormonal Testing & Treatment W/Bio-identical Hormones
	Misaligned Vertebrae	Chiropractic Adjustment
	Outdated Programs	Cookie & Scan Disc (10-20x 1 mo)
	Karma	Karma Transmutation (10-20x 1 mo)
		Basic-Seven-Step-Repair-System For Complete Wellness
Fungus	Simple Carb, Sugar Diet	Diet Lacking Junk Food
	Improper Diet	(Eat Right For Your Blood Type) by Dr. D'Amato Eliminate Sugar & Starches
	Living in the Past	Karma Transmutation (10-20x 1 mo)
		Fungal Cream
		Yogurt with Live Cultures
		Probiotics
		Basic-Seven-Step-Repair-System For Complete Wellness
Gallstones	Anger, Fear	Inner Child (3-5x 3 mo apart)
	Hard Lumps of Anger	Emotional Balancing
		Yin/Yang Balancing
	Broken Meridians	Meridian Repair
	Broken Grids	Grid Repair
	Gallstones	Esoteric Surgery to Remove Stones
	Gallbladder Flush	Edgar Casey
	Vertebrae Misalignment	Chiropractic Adjustment
		Basic-Seven-Step-Repair-System For Complete Wellness
Gas Pains	Fear	Inner Child (3-5x 3 mo apart)
		Emotional Balancing
		Yin/Yang Balancing
	Blocked Chakras	Chakra Balancing
	Improper Diet	(Eat Right For Your Blood Type) by Dr. D'Amato
		Basic-Seven-Step-Repair-System For Complete Wellness
Gastritis	Fear	Inner Child (3-5x 3 mo apart)
		Emotional Balancing
		Yin/Yang Balancing
	Food Intolerances	(Eat Right For Your Blood Type by Dr. D'Amato
	Meridian Breaks	Meridian Repair
	Blocked Sacral/Root Chakra	Chakra Balancing

Problem	Probable Cause	Probable Repairs & Techniques Needed To Resolve the Problem
		Basic-Seven-Step-Repair-System For Complete Wellness
Genitals	Represents Yin/Yang	Yin/Yang Balancing Inner Child (3-5x 3 mo apart)
	Fear of Not Living up to Expectations	Emotional Balancing
	Meridian Block/Break	Meridian Repair
	Blocked Root/Sacral Chakra	Chakra Balancing Basic-Seven-Step-Repair-System For Complete Wellness
Glands	Stagnation of Lymph Fluid	Lymph Technique (3-5x) Exercise, Bike, Walk, etc. Eight Glasses of Water (daily)
	Infection	Possible Antibiotics (see doctor)
	Karma	Karma Transmutation 10-20x 1 mo
	Broken Meridians	Meridian Repair
	Food Intolerance	(Eat Right For Your Blood Type) by Dr. D'Amato
	Misaligned Vertebrae	Chiropractic Adjustment Basic-Seven-Step-Repair-System For Complete Wellness
Glandular Problems	Fear of Moving Forward	Inner Child (3-5x 3 mo apart) Emotional Balancing Yin/Yang Balancing Karma Transmutation 10-20x 1 mo
	Outdated Programs	Cookie & Scan Disc (0-20x 1 mo apart)
	Food Intolerance	(Eat Right For Your Blood Type) by Dr. D'Amato
	Vertebra Misalignment	Chiropractic Adjustment Lymphatic Technique (5x) Lymphatic Massage (bi-monthly) Basic-Seven-Step-Repair-System For Complete Wellness
Gonorrhea	Guilt	Inner Child (3-5x 3 mo apart) Emotional Balancing Yin/Yang Balancing
	Infection	Antibiotics (see doctor)
	Virus/Bacterial	Viral/Bacterial Neutralization Cellular Release DNA Repair Karma Transmutation (10-20x 1 mo) Basic-Seven-Step-Repair-System

Problem	Probable Cause	Probable Repairs & Techniques Needed To Resolve the Problem
		For Complete Wellness
Gout	Anger, Fear	Inner Child (3-5x 3 mo apart)
		Emotional Balancing
		Yin/Yang Balancing
	Broken Meridians	Meridian Repair
	Food Intolerances	(Eat Right For Your Blood Type) by Dr. D'Amato
	Too Much Fat in Diet	Low-Fat Diet
		Cherries (daily)
	Acidic Diet	Alkaline Plant Based Diet
		Basic-Seven-Step-Repair-System For Complete Wellness
Gum Problems	Lack of Trust in One's Decisions	Emotional Balancing
	Inability to Choose Between Alternatives	Yin/Yang Balancing
		Inner Child (3-5x 3 mo apart)
	Poor Dental Hygiene	Tooth Brushing w/Peroxide & Baking Soda
	Broken Meridians	Meridian Repair
	Improper Diet, Not Enough Live Food	(Eat Right For Your Blood Type) by Dr. D'Amato
		Diet Lacking Junk Food
		Basic-Seven-Step-Repair-System For Complete Wellness
Halitosis	Stinking Thinking	Emotional Balancing
		Yin/Yang Balancing
		Inner Child (3-5x 3 mo apart)
	Improper Diet	(Eat Right For Your Blood Type) by Dr. D'Amato
	Stagnation of Body Fluids	Exercise, Bike, Walk, etc.
	Broken Grids	Grid Repair
	Broken Meridians	Meridian Repair
	Lack of Water	Eight Glasses of Water (daily)
		Basic-Seven-Step-Repair-System For Complete Wellness
Hands Problems (See Fingers)	Fear-Unable To Wrap Hands around What is Happening in Your Life	Emotional Balancing
		Yin/Yang Balancing
		Inner Child (3-5x 3 mo apart)
	Broken Meridians	Meridian Repair
	Vertebrae Misalignment	Chiropractic Adjustment
	Spinal Stenosis	EMG
		Massage (2x per mo)

Problem	Probable Cause	Probable Repairs & Techniques Needed To Resolve the Problem
		Physical Therapy
		Spinal Repair
	Broken Crystals	Crystal Repair
	Blocked Fingertip Chakras	Chakra Balancing
		Basic-Seven-Step-Repair-System For Complete Wellness
Hay Fever (See Allergies)	Fear, Guilt Lack of Confidence	Emotional Balancing Yin/Yang Balancing Inner Child (3-5x 3 mo apart)
	Toxic Lymph System	Lymphatic Technique (5x)
	Broken Meridians	Meridian Repair
	Vertebrae Misalignment	Chiropractic Adjustment
	Food Intolerances	(Eat Right For Your Blood Type) by Dr. D'Amato
		Basic-Seven-Step-Repair-System For Complete Wellness
Headaches	Self-Denial, Rigidity and Self-Repression	Yin/Yang Balancing Inner Child (3-5x 3 mo apart)
	Toxic Lymph System	Lymphatic Technique (5x)
	Broken Meridians	Meridian Repair
	Vertebrae Misalignment	Chiropractic Adjustment
	Food Intolerances	(Eat Right For Your Blood Type) by Dr. D'Amato
	Blocked 3rd Eye, Crown Chakras	Chakra Balancing
	Lack of Energetic Hygiene	Energetic Hygiene
		Basic-Seven-Step-Repair-System For Complete Wellness
Heart Problems Cardiac (See Blood)	Following Head, not Heart	Compassion Emotional Balancing
	Lacking Joy	Yin/Yang Balancing Inner Child (3-5x 3 mo apart)
	Cords Strangling Heart	Cut Cords
	Clogged Arteries	Cardiac Repair (10-12x's)
	Broken Grids	Grid Repair
	Broken Meridians	Meridian Repair
	Blocked Chakras	Chakra Balancing
	Body Energetically Blocked	Striking I & II
	Empty Gas Tank	Prana Tube Filling
		Yohimbe in Juice (5 drops, morning)
		EFA (4-6 grams, daily)
		Red Yeast Rice
		Polycosanal (250 mg)

Problem	Probable Cause	Probable Repairs & Techniques Needed To Resolve the Problem
		Baby Aspirin (1x, daily)
		Lipoic Acid (100 mg, 2x daily)
		No Flush Niacin (500 mg)
	Junk Food	Diet Lacking Junk Food
	Acidic Diet	Alkaline Diet Is Key
		(Eat Right For Your Blood Type) by Dr. D'Amato
	Lack of Exercise	Tai-Chi, Qigong, Walk, Bike
		Jasmine Tea
		Energetic Hygiene
		Basic-Seven-Step-Repair-System For Complete Wellness
Heartburn	Fear	Inner Child (3-5x 3 mo apart)
		Emotional Balancing
		Yin/Yang Balancing
	Broken Meridians	Meridian Repair
	Acidic Diet	Alkaline Diet Is Key
	Hiatal Hernia	Weight Loss (see doctor)
	Blocked Heart Chakra	Chakra Balancing
	Misaligned Vertebrae	Chiropractic Adjustment
	Food Intolerances	(Eat Right For Your Blood Type) by Dr. D'Amato
		Basic-Seven-Step-Repair-System For Complete Wellness
Hemorrhoids (Anorectal Bleeding)	Fear, Anger, Exhaustion	Inner Child (3-5x 3 mo apart)
		Emotional Balancing
		Yin/Yang Balancing
	Blocked Chakras	Chakra Balancing
	Acidic Diet	Alkaline Diet
	Misaligned Sacral Vertebrae	Chiropractic Adjustment
	Meridian Block/Break	Meridian Repair
		Basic-Seven-Step-Repair-System For Complete Wellness
Hepatitis	Fear, Anger	Inner Child (3-5x 3 mo apart)
		Emotional Balancing
		Yin/Yang Balancing
	Virus	Virus Neutralization (3x)
		Cellular Release (3x)
	Broken Grids	Grid Repair
	Blocked Chakras	Chakra Balancing
	Meridian Block/Break	Meridian Repair
		Basic-Seven-Step-Repair-System For Complete Wellness

Problem	Probable Cause	Probable Repairs & Techniques Needed To Resolve the Problem
Hernias	Unwanted Thoughts & Mental Arguments	Inner Child (3-5x 3mo apart)
		Yin/Yang Balancing
	Stress, Strain	Emotional Balancing
	Broken Grids	Grid Repair
	Meridian Block/Break	Meridian Repair
	Rupture in Stomach Wall	Health Program
		Limited lifting (<5 lbs for 6 weeks after repair)
		No driving (1 wk after repair)
	Blocked Chakras	Chakra Balancing
	Outdated Concepts	Cookie & Scan Disc (10-20x 1 mo)
		Basic-Seven-Step-Repair-System For Complete Wellness
Herpes	Guilt	Inner Child (3-5x 3 mo apart)
	Excess Stress	Yin/Yang Balancing
	Exposure to Cold Sores	Emotional Balancing
		Living in the NOW
	Underlying Virus	Lysine (500mg daily)
		Cellular Release (3x)
		Virus Neutralization (3x)
	Too much Sun	Sunburn Precautions
	Spicy Foods	Spicy Food Elimination
	Acidic System & Diet	Alkaline Diet Is Key
		Alka-Seltzer (3 days)
		Cookie & Scan Disc (10-20x 1 mo)
		Bach Flower Honeysuckle & Mimulus (half bottle, 2 days in a row)
		Eight Glasses of Water (daily)
		Basic-Seven-Step-Repair-System For Complete Wellness
Hip Problems	Fear	Inner Child (3-5x 3 mo apart)
	Belief in the Calendar and Old Age	Yin/Yang Balancing
		Emotional Balancing
	Fear of Death	
	Stuck In Place	Cookie & Scan Disc (10-20x)
	Misaligned Vertebra	Chiropractic Adjustment
	Meridian Block/Break	Meridian Repair
	Blocked Chakra	Chakra Balancing
	Broken Grids	Grid Repair
		Basic-Seven-Step-Repair-System For Complete Wellness
Hives	Fear	Inner Child (3-5x 3 mo apart)

Problem	Probable Cause	Probable Repairs & Techniques Needed To Resolve the Problem
(See Rash)	What is Under Your Skin?	Yin/Yang Balancing
		Emotional Balancing
	Need Love & Attention Love	Love Technique w/all Others
	Clearing Through Skin	Regular Salt Baths (2 cups to tub)
	Food Intolerances	(Eat Right For Your Blood Type) by Dr. D'Amato
		Basic-Seven-Step-Repair-System For Complete Wellness
Holding Fluids	Fear of Losing Something	Inner Child (3-5x 3 mo apart)
		Yin/Yang Balancing
		Emotional Balancing
	Total Body Energetically	Striking I & II
		Blocked
	Cords Strangling Heart, Keeping it from Pumping Efficiently	Cord Cutting
	Broken Grids	Grid Repair
	Meridian Block/Break	Meridian Repair
	Toxic Lymph System	Lymph Technique (10x)
		Basic-Seven-Step-Repair-System For Complete Wellness
Hyperactivity	Fear, Panic	Inner Child (3-5x 3 mo apart)
		Yin/Yang Balancing
		Emotional Balancing
	Blueprint Imbalance	Blueprint Restoration
		Cookie & Scan Disc (10-20x 1 mo)
	Thyroid Imbalance	See Doctor
		Chemical Balancing
	Too Much Caffeine	Eliminate Caffeine
		Bach Flower Rescue Remedy (daily)
		Basic-Seven-Step-Repair-System For Complete Wellness
Hyperglycemia	Emotional Imbalance	Emotional Balancing
	Living in the Past	Cookie & Scan Disc (10-20x 1 mo)
		Inner Child (3-5x 3 mo apart)
		Yin/Yang Balancing
	Meridian Block/Break	Meridian Repair
	High Carbohydrate Diet	High Protein Diet
		(Eat Right For Your Blood Type) by Dr. D'Amato
	Lack of Exercise	Qigong, Tai-Chi, Walk, Bike
		Basic-Seven-Step-Repair-System For Complete Wellness

Problem	Probable Cause	Probable Repairs & Techniques Needed To Resolve the Problem
Hypertension See high blood pressure	Fear	Inner Child (3-5x 3 mo apart)
	Emotional Challenge	Emotional Balancing
		Yin/Yang Balancing
	Clogged Arteries	Cardiac Repair (10-12x)
		Yohimbe in Juice (5 drops, morning)
	Acidic Diet	Alkaline Diet Is Key (Eat Right For Your Blood Type) by Dr. D'Amato
	Lack of Exercise	Exercise, Tai-Chi, Qigong, Basic-Seven-Step-Repair-System For Complete Wellness
Hyperthyroidism	Not On Your Path	Path Meditation
	Not Expressing Creatively	Path Execution w/Spiritual Counseling
	Not Doing What You Want	Yin/Yang Balancing
	Putting Everyone Else First	Inner Child (3-5x 3 mo apart)
		Emotional Balancing
	Not Being True To Yourself	Cookie & Scan Disc (10-20x 1 mo)
	Excessive Hormone Release	Endocrine Repair
	Chemical Imbalance	Chemical Balancing
	Too Much Caffeine	Caffeine Reduction
	Food Intolerance	(Eat Right For Your Blood Type) by Dr. D'Amato
	Need Detoxification	Live Foods
		Basic-Seven-Step-Repair-System For Complete Wellness
Hypothalamus Governs Endocrine	Feelings of Rage, Insecurity Sadness, Anxiety	Inner Child (3-5x, 1 mo apart)
		Yin/Yang Balancing
		Emotional Balancing
	Lack of Love	Love Meditation (sending pink light through Chakras w/Love Program)
	Endocrine Damage	Endocrine Repair
	Meridian Block/Break	Meridian Repair
	Broken Grids	Grid Repair
	Blocked Crown, Heart Chakras	Chakra Balancing
	Outdated Programs	Cookie & Scan Disc (10x 1 mo apart)
	Blocked Arteries	Cardiac Repair (10-12x)
		Basic-Seven-Step-Repair-System For Complete Wellness
Hypothyroidism	Not Being on Your Path	Path Meditation
	Not Expressing Creatively	Path Execution w/Spiritual Counseling
	Not Doing What You Want	Yin/Yang Balancing
	Putting Everyone Else First	Inner Child (3-5x 3 mo apart)

Problem	Probable Cause	Probable Repairs & Techniques Needed To Resolve the Problem
	(When Is It My Turn?)	Emotional Balancing
	Be True To Yourself	Cookie & Scan Disc (10-20x)
	Eating or Drinking Soy	Diet Lacking Soy
	Lack of Female Hormones	Bio-identical Hormones
	Lack of Human Growth Hormone	Human Growth Hormone
	Injuries to the Pituitary & Pineal Glands	Endocrine Repair Love Meditation (w/pink light)
	Broken Grids	Grid Repair
	Meridian Block/Break	Meridian Repair
	Lack of Exercise	Tai-Chi, Qigong, Walk, Bike
	Cervical Injuries	Crystal Repair Spinal Repair
	Misaligned Vertebrae	Chiropractic Adjustment
	Lack of Iodinated Salt	Sea Salts
	Chemical Imbalance	Chemical Balancing
	Blocked Throat, Thymus Chakras	Chakra Balancing Basic-Seven-Step-Repair-System For Complete Wellness
Impotence See Cholesterol See Blood	Sexual Pressure	Yin/Yang Balancing
	Guilt, Fear	Inner Child (3-5x 3 mo apart)
	Unresolved Issues w/Females	Emotional Balancing
	Outdated Programs	Cookie & Scan Disc (10-12x 1 mo)
	Meridian Block/Break	Meridian Repair
	Broken Grids	Grid Repair
	Blocked Sacral, Root Chakras	Chakra Balancing
	Plaque or Clogged Arteries	Cardiac Repair (10-12x) Yohimbe in Juice (5 drops daily) Jasmine Tea
	Total Body Energetically Blocked	Red Yeast Rice (500 mg at bedtime) Striking I & II
	Acidic Diet	Alkaline Diet Is Key
	Poor Circulation	Exercise, Tai-Chi, Qigong, etc Co-Q 10
	Blocked Urethra w/Minerals from Lack of Sex	Ejaculation
	Low Testosterone Count	Bio-identical Hormone Replacement Basic-Seven-Step-Repair-System For Complete Wellness
Incontinence (See Lower Back)	Emotional Imbalance	Emotional Balancing
	Fear	Inner Child (3-5x 3 mo apart) Yin/Yang Balancing
	Weak Kegel Muscles	Kegel Exercises
	Blocked Chakras	Chakra Balancing

Problem	Probable Cause	Probable Repairs & Techniques Needed To Resolve the Problem
	Broken Crystals	Crystal Repair
	Vertebra Misalignment	Chiropractic Adjustments
		Basic-Seven-Step-Repair-System For Complete Wellness
Incurable Injury, Illness	Not Speaking to the Solution, With God, All Things are Possible	Appreciation for God's Healing Faith/Trust
	Illness Starts on Spiritual Plane	Meditation on the Inner Man
		Inner Child
		Emotional Balancing
		Yin/Yang Balancing
		Basic-Seven-Step-Repair-System For Complete Wellness
		Other Based on Consultation
Indigestion	Fear	Emotional Balancing
		Yin/Yang Balancing
		Inner Child (3-5x 3 mo apart)
	Food Intolerance	(Eat Right For Your Blood Type) by Dr. D'Amato
	Acidic Diet	Alkaline Diet Is Key
		Try Food Combining
	Blocked Chakras	Chakra Balancing
	Meridian Block/Break	Meridian Repair
		Basic-Seven-Step-Repair-System For Complete Wellness
Infection (Viral)	Anger Festering	Inner Child (3-5x 3 mo apart)
	Lack of Joy	Yin/Yang Balancing
		Emotional Balancing
		Time to Play
	Thymus Chakra Blocked	Chakra Balancing
	Virus	Virus Neutralization
		Cellular Release
	Meridian Block/Break	Meridian Repair
	Acidic Diet	Alkaline Diet Is Key
	Food Intolerance	(Eat Right For Your Blood Type) by Dr. D'Amato
		Basic-Seven-Step-Repair-System For Complete Wellness
Inflammation	Fear	Emotional Balancing
		Yin/Yang Balancing
		Inner Child (3-5x 3 mo apart)
	Meridian Block/Break	Meridian Repair
	Acidic Diet	Alkaline Diet is key

Problem	Probable Cause	Probable Repairs & Techniques Needed To Resolve the Problem
	Improper Diet	Powdered Ginger in Tea (Eat Right For Your Blood Type) by Dr. D'Amato Basic-Seven-Step-Repair-System For Complete Wellness
Influenza	Fear	Emotional Balancing Yin/Yang Balancing Inner Child (3-5x 3 mo apart)
	Blocked Thymus Chakra	Chakra Balancing
	Virus	Virus Neutralization Cellular Release
	Acidic Diet	Alkaline Diet
	Improper Diet	(Eat Right For Your Blood Type) by Dr. D'Amato Basic-Seven-Step-Repair-System For Complete Wellness
Ingrown Toenail	Fear of Moving Forward	Emotional Balancing Yin/Yang Balancing Inner Child (3-5x 3 mo apart) Toenail Cut by Professional Pedicurist or Podiatrist Basic-Seven-Step-Repair-System For Complete Wellness
Insanity	Major Fear	Emotional Balancing Yin/Yang Balancing Inner Child (3-5x 3 mo apart)
	Entity Possession	Entity Removal (sometimes more than once depending on karma)
	Corded to Entity	Cord Cutting
	Stuck in a Crazy Place	Cookie & Scan Disc (10-20x 1 mo)
	Blueprint Unbalanced	Blueprint Restoration (2-5x)
	Karma	Karma Transmutation (10-20x 1 mo)
	Misunderstanding & Fear of Clairvoyant Gifts (See, Hear And Know Things That Others Do Not)	Develop Comfort with Gifts
	Lack of Serotonin	Sun Exposure (15 min-1 hour, daily)
	Chemical Imbalance	Chemical Balancing
	Unbalanced Crown Chakra	Chakra Balancing Grid Repair Psychiatric Care & Medicine Basic-Seven-Step-Repair-System For Complete Wellness

Problem	Probable Cause	Probable Repairs & Techniques Needed To Resolve the Problem
Insomnia	Fear	Yin/Yang Balancing
		Emotional Balancing
		Inner Child (3-5x 1 mo apart)
	Too much Caffeine	Diet Lacking Coffee, Tea, Chocolate
	Light Disturbance	Sleeping in Darkness
	Lack of Human Growth Hormone	Hormone Replacement
	Pituitary Damage	Endocrine Repair
	Pineal Damage	Endocrine Repair
		Compassion (10x)
	Lack of Melatonin	Melatonin (3x per week)
	Lack of Exercise	Tai-Chi, Yoga, Qigong, Walk, Bike
	Lack of Faith	Trust in God
		Basic-Seven-Step-Repair-System For Complete Wellness
Intestines/Colon	Fear	Emotional Balancing
	Living in the Past	Yin/Yang Balancing
		Inner Child (3-5x 3 mo apart)
	Stuck in the Past	Karma Transmutation (10-20x 1 mo)
		Implant Removal (10-20x 1 mo apart)
	Improper Diet for Your Blood Type	(Eat Right For Your Blood Type) by Dr. D'Amato
	Wheat Intolerance	Wheat Elimination
		Basic-Seven-Step-Repair-System For Complete Wellness
Jaundice (Relates to Liver)	Anger	Yin/Yang Balancing
	Alcohol Abuse	Emotional Balancing
		Inner Child (3-5x 3 mo apart)
	Entity Possession	Entity Removal
	Chemical Imbalance	Chemical Balancing
	Broken Liver, Gallbladder	
	Spleen Meridians	Meridian Repair
	Broken Grids	Grid Repair
	Outdated Cookies	Cookie & Scan Disc (10x)
	Hepatitis	See Doctor
		Virus Neutralization (10x)
		Cellular Release (5x)
		Lymphatic Technique (10x)
		Basic-Seven-Step-Repair-System For Complete Wellness
Jaw Problem (TMJ)	Anger	Yin/Yang Balancing
		Emotional Balancing

Problem	Probable Cause	Probable Repairs & Techniques Needed To Resolve the Problem
		Inner Child (3-5x 3 mo apart)
	Misaligned Vertebrae	Chiropractic Adjustment
	Misaligned Teeth	See Dentist
	Injuries to Cervical Area	Crystal Repair
		Spinal Repair
		Health Program
	Too Much Caffeine	Caffeine Reduction
		Basic-Seven-Step-Repair-System For Complete Wellness
Joints	See Arthritis	
Kidney Problems	FEAR (in capital letters)	Inner Child (3-5x 3 mo apart)
		Yin/Yang Balancing
		Emotional Balancing
	Meridian Block/Break	Meridian Repair
	Empty Batteries	Battery Recharging (bi-weekly)
		Adrenal Supplement
		Salt/Bubble Baths (daily)
	Empty Gas Tank	Prana Tube Filling
	Misaligned Vertebrae	Chiropractic Adjustment
		Basic-Seven-Step-Repair-System For Complete Wellness
Kidney Stones	Fear	Inner Child (3-5x 3 mo apart)
		Yin/Yang Balancing
		Emotional Balancing
	Broken Meridians	Meridian Repair
	Empty Batteries	Battery Recharging
		Regular Salt/Bubble Baths
	Empty Gas Tank	Prana Tube Filling
	Misaligned Vertebrae	Chiropractic Adjustment
	Stone Blockages	Esoteric Surgery to Remove Stones
		Stone Breaker Herbal Tea
		Chanca Piedra
		Basic-Seven-Step-Repair-System For Complete Wellness
Knee Problems	Fear-What Is Holding You Back?	Inner Child (3-5x 3 mo apart)
		Yin/Yang Balancing
		Emotional Balancing
	Broken Crystals	Crystal Repair
	Meridian Block/Break	Meridian Repair
	Broken Grids	Grid Repair
	Cords	Cord Cutting
	Outdated Programs	Cookie & Scan Disc (10x 1 mo apart)

Problem	Probable Cause	Probable Repairs & Techniques Needed To Resolve the Problem
	Misaligned Vertebrae	Chiropractic Adjustments
		Basic-Seven-Step-Repair-System For Complete Wellness
Left Side of Body	Female Side of Body Out-of-Balance	Yin/Yang Balancing
		Emotional Balancing
		Inner Child (3-5x 3 mo apart)
		Basic-Seven-Step-Repair-System For Complete Wellness
		Other Based on Consultation
Leg Problems	Fear (What is Holding You Back?)	Emotional Balancing
		Yin/Yang Balancing
		Inner Child (3-5x 3 mo apart)
	Meridian Block/Break	Meridian Repair
	Broken Crystals	Crystal Repair
	Broken Grids	Grid Repair
	Cords	Cord Cutting
	Outdated Programs	Cookie & Scan Disc (8x 1 mo apart)
	Unresolved Karma	Karma Transmutation (10x 1x mo)
	Spinal Challenge	Spinal Repair
	Misaligned Vertebrae	Chiropractic Adjustment
		Basic-Seven-Step-Repair-System For Complete Wellness
Leukemia	Lack of Love Feeling Hopeless Tired of Life	Love (simultaneous w/each repair)
		Yin/Yang Balancing
		Emotional Balancing
		Inner Child (3-5x 3 mo apart)
	Outdated Programs	Cookie & Scan Disc (10x)
	Cords	Cord Cutting
	Unresolved Karma	Karma Transmutation (10x)
		Cellular Release (8x)
		Basic-Seven-Step-Repair-System For Complete Wellness
Liver Problems	Anger	Yin/Yang Balancing
		Emotional Balancing
		Inner Child (3-5x 3 mo apart)
	Lack of Forgiveness	Forgiveness Technique (10-20x)
	Outdated Programs	Cookie & Scan Disc (10x)
	Meridian Block/Break	Meridian Repair
	Broken Grids	Grid Repair
	Unresolved Karma	Karma Transmutation (10-20x 1x mo)
	Misaligned Vertebrae	Chiropractic Adjustment

Problem	Probable Cause	Probable Repairs & Techniques Needed To Resolve the Problem
		Basic-Seven-Step-Repair-System For Complete Wellness
Lung Problems	Grief, Sadness	Emotional Balancing
		Inner Child (3-5x 3 mo apart)
		Yin/Yang Balancing
	Lung Meridian Block/Break	Meridian Repair
	Broken Grids	Grid Repair
	Misaligned Vertebrae	Chiropractic Adjustment
	Cords Strangling Heart	Cord Cutting
	Outdated Programs	Cookie & Scan Disc (10x)
	Karma	Karma Transmutation
	Lack of Forgiveness	Forgiveness
	Blocked Throat, Thymus, Heart Chakras	Chakra Balancing
	Total Body Energetically Blocked	Striking I & II
	Viral or Bacteria Infection	Virus Neutralization (3-8x) Cellular Release (3-8x) Basic-Seven-Step-Repair-System For Complete Wellness
Lupus	Grief, Hopelessness	Emotional Balancing Yin/Yang Balancing Inner Child (3-5x 3 mo apart)
	Outdated Programs	Cookie & Scan Disc (10x)
	Virus	Virus Neutralization (10x) Cellular Release (8x)
	Karma	Karma Transmutation (10-20x 1x mo)
	Lack of Joy	Joy Filled Activities (2 per week)
	Lack of exercise	Qigong, Tai-Chi, Yoga, Bike,
	Empty Gas Tank	Prana Tube Filling
	Dead Batteries	Battery Recharging (bi-monthly) Basic-Seven-Step-Repair-System For Complete Wellness
Lymph Problems	Lack of Joy & Love	Emotional Balancing Inner Child (3-5x 3 mo apart) Yin/Yang Balancing Love (simultaneous w/each repair)
	Lack of Forgiveness	Forgiveness Technique (10-20x)
	Stagnation from Lack of Exercise	Bike, Qigong, Tai-Chi, Weight Training
	Underarms Blocked by Deodorant	Baby Powder, Baking Soda
	Lymph Fluid Stagnation	Lymphatic Technique (10x)

Problem	Probable Cause	Probable Repairs & Techniques Needed To Resolve the Problem
	Total Body Energetically Blocked	Striking I & II Basic-Seven-Step-Repair-System For Complete Wellness
Migraine Headache	Overextension of Abilities Fear of Not Getting Enough Done	Relaxation, Trust in God Simplification of Life Emotional Balancing Yin/Yang Balancing Inner Child (3-5x 3 mo apart)
	Meridian Block/Break Blocked Crown, 3rd Eye Chakra	Meridian Repair Chakra Balancing
	Cording Misaligned Vertebrae Food Intolerance	Cord Cutting Chiropractic Adjustments Eat Right For Your Blood Type by Dr. D'Amato
	Broken Crystals In Head Area	Crystal Repair
		Basic-Seven-Step-Repair-System For Complete Wellness
Miscarriage	Fear	Emotional Balancing Inner Child (3-5x 3 mo apart) Yin/Yang Balancing
	Meridian Block/Break Blocked Chakras in Lower Body	Meridian Repair Chakra Balancing
	Misaligned Vertebrae Unresolved Karma Hormonal Imbalance	Chiropractic Adjustment Karma Transmutation (10-20x 1x mo) See Anti-Aging Specialist for Bio-Identical Hormones
	Outdated Programs	Cookie & Scan Disc (10x) Basic-Seven-Step-Repair-System For Complete Wellness
Mononucleosis	Anger-Lacking Love	Love simultaneous w/each technique Inner Child (3-5x 3 mo apart) Emotional Balancing Yin/Yang Balancing
	Blocked Thymus Chakra Acidic Diet Food Intolerances	Chakra Balancing Alkaline Diet is key (Eat Right For Your Blood Type) by Dr. D'Amato
	Lack of Rest Lack of Exercise & Sun	Eight Hours of Sleep (daily) Qigong, Tai-Chi, Walk, Bike

Problem	Probable Cause	Probable Repairs & Techniques Needed To Resolve the Problem
		Basic-Seven-Step-Repair-System For Complete Wellness
Motion Sickness (Car/Boat)	Fear	Emotional Balancing Yin/Yang Balancing Inner Child (3-5x 3 mo apart) Basic-Seven-Step-Repair-System For Complete Wellness
Multiple Sclerosis (See Heart Problems/ Cardiac)	Fear Rigid Thoughts	Emotional Balancing Yin/Yang Balancing Inner Child (3-5x 3 mo apart)
	Unresolved Karma Virus	Karma Transmutation (10x 1 mo apart) Virus Neutralization (10x) Cellular Release (10x & Specialist)
	Imbalance In Brain Wave Frequency Chakra Blocks Heart Strangled by Cords Holes in Grid System Meridian Block/Break Body Energetically Blocked Depleted Batteries Empty Gas Tank Broken Crystals Heart Challenge	DNA Repair (3-5x) Brain Balancing Chakra Balancing Cord Cutting (1-2x) Grid Repair (2-4x) Meridian Repair (2x) Striking I & II (1-2x) Battery Recharging (monthly) Prana Tube Filling Crystal Repair (2-3x) Cardiac Repair (10x 2x per week) Etheric Organ Replacement (heart)
	Need Pain Relief	Aqua Aura Channeled through Gateways (3x a year)
	Food Intolerance	(Eat Right For Your Blood Type) by Dr. D'Amato
	Lack of Exercise	Qigong, Tai-Chi, Walk, Bike, Jasmine Tea
	Damaged Nerve Endings Nutritional Deficiencies	B-12 Injections (monthly) Multi-Mineral & Vitamin Supplement Vitamin D (400 mg daily) Bach Flower Vine (1 dropper daily) Basic-Seven-Step-Repair-System For Complete Wellness
Myocardial Infarction	See Heart Attack	
Narcolepsy	Fear	Inner Child (3-5x 3 mo apart) Emotional Balancing

Problem	Probable Cause	Probable Repairs & Techniques Needed To Resolve the Problem
		Yin/Yang Balancing
	Empty Batteries	Battery Recharging
	Empty Gas Tank	Prana Tube Filling
	Empty Mental & Emotional Reserves	Mental & Emotional Reserve Recharging
	Broken Grids	Grid Repair
	Meridian Block/Break	Meridian Repair
	Blocked Chakras	Chakra Balancing
		Basic-Seven-Step-Repair-System For Complete Wellness
Nausea	Fear	Inner Child (3-5x 3 mo apart)
		Emotional Balancing
		Yin/Yang Balancing
	Blocked/Broken Spleen & Gallbladder Meridians	Meridian Repair
	Possible Kidney Stones	Esoteric Surgery to Remove Stones
	Food Poisoning	Natural Processing of Poison
		Virus Neutralization
	Parasites	Holistic Parasite Remedy
	Food Intolerance	(Eat Right For Your Blood Type) by Dr. D'Amato
	Hormonal Imbalance	See Anti-Aging Specialist
		Basic-Seven-Step-Repair-System For Complete Wellness
Neck	Lack of Forgiveness of Self & Others	Forgiveness Technique (10-20x)
Cervical Spine	Cervical Radiculopathy	MRI-Spinal Repair (10x)
	Spinal Stenosis	Rehabilitative & Physical Therapy
		Peanut Oil Spinal Massage to Break Up Scar Tissue
		Stretching Exercises (daily)
		Qigong, Tai Chi
		Trigger Point Injections (for pain)
		Health Program
	Broken Crystals	Crystal Repair
	Meridian Block/Break	Meridian Repair
	Broken Grids	Grid Repair
	Misaligned Vertebrae	Chiropractic Adjustment
	Food Intolerances	(Eat Right For Your Blood Type) by Dr. D'Amato
		Alkaline Diet
		Basic-Seven-Step-Repair-System For Complete Wellness

Problem	Probable Cause	Probable Repairs & Techniques Needed To Resolve the Problem
Nervous Breakdown	Fear, Anxiety	Emotional Balancing
		Yin/Yang Balancing
		Inner Child (3-5x 3 mo apart)
		Trust in God
	Unbalanced Blueprint	Blueprint Restoration (1-2x)
	Outdated Programs	Cookie & Scan Disc (10-20x)
	Karma	Karma Transmutation (10-20x 1x mo)
		Basic-Seven-Step-Repair-System
		For Complete Wellness
Nose Bleeds	Lack of Love	Emotional Balancing
		Inner child (3-5x 3 mo apart)
		Yin/Yang Balancing
		Love (simultaneous w/each repair)
	Karma	Karma Transmutation (10-20x)
		Basic-Seven-Step-Repair-System
		For Complete Wellness
Nose Runny	Needs Emotional Balancing	Emotional Balancing
		Inner Child (3-5x 3 mo apart)
		Local Honey (1-3 tbsp, daily)
	Toxic Lymph System	Lymphatic Technique (3-5x)
	Food Intolerance	(Eat Right For Your Blood Type)
	Allergies	by Dr. D'Amato
	Acidic Diet	Alkaline Diet
	Chemical Imbalance	Chemical Balancing
		Basic-Seven-Step-Repair-System
		For Complete Wellness
Nose Stuffy	Lacking Self-Esteem	Love simultaneous w/each technique
	Irritation	Emotional Balancing
		Inner Child (3-5x 3 mo apart)
		Yin/Yang Balancing
		Local Honey (1-3 tbsp, daily)
	Meridian Block/Break	Meridian Repair
	Broken Grids	Grid Repair
	Blocked Occipital, 3rd eye & Throat Chakras	Chakra Balancing
	Allergies	(Eat Right For Your Blood Type)
	Food Intolerances	by Dr. D'Amato
	Chemical Imbalance	Chemical Balancing
		Basic-Seven-Step-Repair-System
		For Complete Wellness
Numbness	Painful Love Life	Inner Child (3-5x 3 mo apart)
	Withdrawing Love	Emotional Balancing

Problem	Probable Cause	Probable Repairs & Techniques Needed To Resolve the Problem
		Yin/Yang Balancing
	Misaligned Vertebrae Pressing on Nerve	Chiropractic Adjustments
	Meridian Block/Break	Meridian Repair
	Lack of Blood Flow & Energy to Area	Massage (regularly)
	Radiculopathy	EMG-Spinal Repair (4-6x)
		Physical Therapy
		Health Program
	Broken Grids	Grid Repair
		Basic-Seven-Step-Repair-System For Complete Wellness
Osteoporosis	Lack of Emotional Support	Inner Child (3-5x 3 mo apart)
		Emotional Balancing
		Yin/Yang Balancing
	Acidic Diet	Alkaline Diet Is Key
		Weight Bearing Exercises
		Plant Based Diet
	Lack of Calcium & Vitamin D	Calcium & Vitamin D Supplements
		Glucosamine Sulfate
		Fish Oil
		EFA
		Eight Glasses of Water (daily)
		Basic-Seven-Step-Repair-System For Complete Wellness
Ovaries	Lonely & Lack of Love	Love Technique Simultaneous w/all
	Fear of Sexual Role	Inner Child (3-5x 3 mo apart)
		Emotional Balancing
		Yin/Yang Balancing
	Hormonal Imbalance	Bio-Identical Hormones See Anti-Aging Specialist
	Blocked Sacral Chakra	Chakra Balancing
	Meridian Block/Break	Meridian Repair
	Outdated Programs	Cookie & Scan Disc (10x 1x mo)
	Endocrine Problems or Breaks in Connections	Endocrine Repair See Endocrinologist
	Misaligned Vertebrae	Chiropractic Adjustment
	Broken Grids	Grid Repair
		Basic-Seven-Step-Repair-System For Complete Wellness
Overweight	Fear	Emotional Balancing
	Protection from Change & Unwanted Influences	Inner Child (3-5x 3 mo apart)
		Yin/Yang Balancing

Problem	Probable Cause	Probable Repairs & Techniques Needed To Resolve the Problem
	Lack of Confidence	
	Acidic Diet	Alkaline Diet
	Food Intolerances	(Eat Right For Your Blood Type) by Dr. D'Amato
	Lack of Exercise	Qigong, Tai-Chi, Bike, Walk Weight Training, Aerobic Exercise Love Technique Simultaneous w/All Basic-Seven-Step-Repair-System For Complete Wellness
Pain	Have Been Given a Reason to Turn to God for Help	Prayer, Meditation on Inner Man & God's Guidance
	Not On Your Path	Path Meditation, Gut Feel, Intuition, Spiritual Counseling
	Emotional Imbalance	Emotional Balancing Yin/Yang Balancing Inner Child (3-5x 3 mo apart)
	Misaligned Vertebrae	Chiropractic Adjustment
	Search for Cause of Pain	See Pain Doctor
	Blocked Chakras	Chakra Balancing
	Clogged Meridians	Striking I & II
	Stress	All of the Above Plus Yoga, Meditation Basic-Seven-Step-Repair-System For Complete Wellness
Pancreas	Self-Denial of Joy, Rigid Judgment, Self-Repression	Inner Child (3-5x 3 mo apart
		Yin/Yang Balancing
	Incorrect Expression of Ego	Emotional Balancing
	Meridian Block/Break	Meridian Repair
	Simple Carb Diet	Plant Based Diet
	Blocked Solar Plexus, Heart Chakras	Chakra Balancing
	Mineral Imbalance	Multi-Mineral Supplements Chemical Balancing Basic-Seven-Step-Repair-System For Complete Wellness
Pancreatitis	Lack of Joy & Love	Inner Child (3-5x 3 mo apart) Emotional Balancing Yin/Yang Balancing Love Tech Simultaneously w/All
	Meridian Block/Break	Meridian Repair
	Outdated Programs	Cookie & Scan Disc (10x) (Remove Programs Related to Alcoholism)

Problem	Probable Cause	Probable Repairs & Techniques Needed To Resolve the Problem
	Karma	Karma Transmutation (10x 1x mo)
	High Carbohydrate Diet	Diet of Protein, Vegetables, Fruit
	Lack of Exercise	Qigong, Tai-Chi, Walk, Bike
	Alcoholism	Implant Removal
		Basic-Seven-Step-Repair-System For Complete Wellness
Paralyzed Arms		
Left (See Fingers)	Must Learn To Receive	Emotional Balancing
Right (See Fingers)	Must Learn To Give	Yin/Yang Balancing
(See Paralysis)		Inner Child (3-5x 3 mo apart)
	Karma	Karma Transmutation (10-20x 1x mo)
	Stuck in Place	Cookie & Scan Disc (10x 1 mo apart)
	Broken Crystals	Crystal Repair
	Spinal Cord Damage	Spinal Repair
	Radiculopathy	EMG
		Physical Therapy
	Misaligned Vertebrae	Chiropractic Adjustment
	Spinal Stenosis	Peanut Oil Spinal Massage (weekly)
		See Arthritis
		Basic-Seven-Step-Repair-System For Complete Wellness
Paralysis	Major Fear of Known Things (A Way to Escape)	Inner Child (3-5x 3 mo apart)
		Emotional Balancing
		Yin/Yang Balancing
	Broken Grids	Grid Repair
	Meridian Block/Break	Meridian Repair
	Broken Crystals	Crystal Repair
	Empty Gas Tank	Prana Tube Filling
	Dead Batteries	Battery Recharging
	Empty Emotional & Mental Reserves	Emotional & Mental Reserve Recharging
	Stuck in Old Programs	Cookie & Scan Disc (10x)
	Karma	Karma Transmutation (10x)
	Spinal Cord Repair	Spinal Repair
		Basic-Seven-Step-Repair-System For Complete Wellness
Parasites	Not Owning Your Own Power	Emotional Balancing
		Yin/Yang Balancing
		Inner Child (3-5x 3 mo apart)
	Outdated Programs	Cookie & Scan Disc (10x)
	Karma	Karma Transmutation (10x 1x mo)
	Sleeping w/Pets	De-Worming of Self & Pets (1 mo, with holistic remedy,

Problem	Probable Cause	Probable Repairs & Techniques Needed To Resolve the Problem
		then 3 days before & 3 days after full moon to kill remaining eggs
	Letting Animals Kiss You on Lips	Turning of Head Thorough Washing of Mouth
	Unclean Fruits & Veggies	Thorough Washing
	Parasites on Hands	Washing Hands after Bathroom Usage Have Tap Water Checked For Parasites Basic-Seven-Step-Repair-System For Complete Wellness
Peptic Ulcer	Fear, Lack of Self Esteem	Inner Child (3-5x 3 mo apart) Emotional Balancing Yin/Yang Balancing
	H. Pylori Virus	Antibiotics Virus Neutralization (3x) Cellular Release (3x)
	Poor Dental Hygiene	Brushing & Flossing (regularly) Mouthwash Daily
	Outdated Programs	Cookie & Scan Disc (10x)
	Acidic Diet	Alkaline Diet Is Key Basic-Seven-Step-Repair-System For Complete Wellness
Petit Mal Epilepsy	Fear	Emotional Balancing Inner Child Yin/Yang Balancing
	Meridian Block/Break	Meridian Repair
	Feeling Overwhelmed by Responsibility	Elm Bach Flower Remedy
	Major Broken Grids Especially In Head/Brain	Major Grid Repair (3-4x)
	Electromagnetic Wounds	Wound Sealing Health Program
	Adrenaline Burnout	Battery Recharging Adrenaline Supplementation Walking/Running Recharges The Adrenals
	Needs Water Element	Bath In Sea Salts Regularly Basic-Seven-Step-Repair-System For Complete Wellness
Phlebitis	Fear, Feeling Discouraged	Emotional Balancing Yin/Yang Balancing Inner Child (3-5x 3 mo apart)
	Karma	Karma Transmutation (10-20x 1x mo)
	Old Programming	Cookie & Scan Disc (10x 1 mo apart)

Problem	Probable Cause	Probable Repairs & Techniques Needed To Resolve the Problem
	Clots & Plaque In Veins	Cardiac Repair (5-10x)
	Meridian Block/Break	Meridian Repair
	Broken Crystals	Crystal Repair
	Broken Grids	Grid Repair
	Body Energetically Blocked	Striking I & II
		Basic-Seven-Step-Repair-System For Complete Wellness
Piles	See Hemorrhoids	
Pink Eye	Not Wanting To See	Emotional Balancing
	Anger over Situation	Yin/Yang Balancing
		Inner Child (3-5x 3 mo apart)
	Meridian Block/Break	Meridian Repair
	Broken Grids	Grid Repair
	Karma	Karma Transmutation (10-20x 1x mo)
	Virus	Virus Neutralization (3x)
		Cellular Release (3x 3 mo apart)
		Basic-Seven-Step-Repair-System For Complete Wellness
Pineal Gland (Relates to Inner Sight)	Not on Enlightenment Path	Spiritual Counseling
	Blocked 3rd Eye & Occipital Chakras	Chakra Balancing
	Meridian Block/Break	Meridian Repair
	Outdated Programming	Cookie & Scan Disc (10x 1 mo apart)
	Not Enough Love	Love Meditation w/Pink Light Running Through All Chakras
		Love Technique simultaneously w/All)
	Endocrine Challenge	See Endocrinologist & Anti-Aging Specialist
	Accident?	Endocrine Repair
	Karma	Karma Transmutation (10-20x 1x mo)
	Broken Pineal Crystal	Crystal Repair
		Basic-Seven-Step-Repair-System For Complete Wellness
Pituitary Gland	Body, Mind & Spirit out of Balance	Emotional Balancing
		Yin/Yang Balancing
		Inner Child (3-5x 3 mo apart)
	Damaged Pituitary	Endocrine Repair
	Accident?	Human Growth Hormone
		See Endocrinologist & Anti-Aging Specialist
	Blocked 3rd Eye, Occipital, & Crown Chakras	Chakra Balancing

Problem	Probable Cause	Probable Repairs & Techniques Needed To Resolve the Problem
	Meridian Block/Break	Meridian Repair
	Outdated Programming	Cookie & Scan Disc (10x 1 mo apart)
	Not Enough Love	Love Meditation w/Pink Light Running Through All Chakras
		Love Tech (simultaneous w/each repair)
	Broken Pituitary Crystal	Crystal Repair
	Lack of Mental & Emotional Discipline	Mental & Emotional Discipline
		Basic-Seven-Step-Repair-System For Complete Wellness
Pneumonia	Grief, Sadness	Emotional Balancing
		Inner Child (3-5x 3 mo apart)
		Yin/Yang Balancing
	Meridian Block/Break	Meridian Repair
	Broken Grids	Grid Repair
	Misaligned Vertebrae	Chiropractic Adjustment
	Cords Strangling Heart	Cord Cutting
	Outdated Programs	Cookie & Scan Disc (10x)
	Karma	Karma Transmutation (10-20x)
	Lack of Forgiveness	Forgiveness Technique (10-20)
	Blocked Throat, Thymus & Heart Chakras	Chakra Balancing
	Body Energetically Blocked	Striking I & II
	Virus	Antibiotics
		Bed Rest
		Virus Neutralization (3x)
		Cellular Release (3x 3 mo apart)
		Basic-Seven-Step-Repair-System For Complete Wellness
Post-Nasal Drip	Victim Mentality	Emotional Balancing
	Sadness, Grief, Weeping Inside	Yin/Yang Balancing
		Inner Child (3-5x 3 mo apart)
	Outdated Programs	Cookie & Scan Disc (10x 1 mo apart)
	Lack of Forgiveness	Forgiveness Technique (8x 1 wk apart)
	Blocked Occipital Chakra	Chakra Balancing
	Meridian Block/Break	Meridian Repair
	Broken Crystal	Crystal Repair
	Sinus Infections	Antibiotics
		Virus Neutralization (10x)
		Cellular Release (3x)
	Toxic Lymph System	Lymphatic Technique (5x)
	Food Intolerance	(Eat Right For Your Blood Type) by Dr. D'Amato
		Basic-Seven-Step-Repair-System

Problem	Probable Cause	Probable Repairs & Techniques Needed To Resolve the Problem
		For Complete Wellness
Premenstrual Syndrome (PMS)	Not Owning & Claiming Own Power	Emotional Balancing
		Inner Child (3-5x 1 mo apart)
	Dislike Female Part of Self	Yin/Yang Balancing
	Outdated Programs	Cookie & Scan Disc (10x 1 mo apart)
	Blocked Sacral Chakra	Chakra Balancing
	Meridian Block/Break	Meridian Repair
	Broken Crystals in Spine	Crystal Repair
	Misaligned Vertebrae	Chiropractic Adjustment
	Cords	Cord Cutting
		Basic-Seven-Step-Repair-System For Complete Wellness
Prostate Problems (Masculine Principal)	Fear of Aging	Emotional Balancing
		Yin/Yang Balancing
		Inner Child (3-5x 1 mo apart)
	Lack of Sex Creates Mineral Blockages in Urethra	Enjoy Regular Sex
	Plaque & Cholesterol Blockages	Cardiac Repair (10x-12x)
	Meridian Block/Break	Meridian Repair
	Broken Grids	Grid Repair
	Blocked Sacral/Root Chakras	Chakra Balancing
	Outdated Programs	Cookie & Scan Disc (10x 1 mo apart)
		Basic-Seven-Step-Repair-System For Complete Wellness
Psoriasis (See Skin Problems) (See Arthritis)	Fear, Emotional Insecurity	Inner Child (3-5x 1 mo apart)
	Depression	Emotional Balancing
	Unresolved Hurt Feelings	Yin/Yang Balancing
		Forgiveness Technique (10x)
	Viral/Bacterial Associated with Ankylosing Spondylitis (Klebsiella Bacterial Strain) & (Psoriasis Arthritis)	Virus Neutralization
		Cellular Release
		DNA Repair
		Indigo Naturalis Creme
	Blueprint Damage	Blueprint Restoration
	Food Intolerances	Diet Lacking Grains
		Basic-Seven-Step-Repair-System For Complete Wellness
Pyorrhea (Periodontitis)	Self-Hatred & Anger at Lack of Decision Making Skills	Emotional Balancing
		Yin/Yang Balancing
		Inner Child (3-5x 3 mo apart)
	Poor Dental Hygiene	Brushing & Flossing (regularly)
		Mouth Rinse of 1 oz Hydrogen

Problem	Probable Cause	Probable Repairs & Techniques Needed To Resolve the Problem
		Peroxide & 3 oz Water (2x daily)
	Meridian Block/Break	Meridian Repair
	Broken Grids	Grid Repair
		Basic-Seven-Step-Repair-System For Complete Wellness
Rash	What is Under Your Skin?	Emotional Balancing Yin/Yang Balancing Inner Child (3-5x 3 mo apart)
	Food Intolerances	(Eat Right For Your Blood Type) by Dr. D'Amato
	Allergies	See Specialist Regular Sea Salt Baths (2 cups) Basic-Seven-Step-Repair-System For Complete Wellness
Respiratory Challenges	Grief, Sadness	Yin/Yang Balancing Inner Child (3-5x 1 mo apart)
	Meridian Block/Break	Meridian Repair
	Blocked Heart & Thymus Chakras	Chakra Balancing
	Cords Strangling Heart	Cord Cutting
	Misaligned Vertebra	Chiropractic Adjustments
	Broken Crystals in Spine	Crystal Repair Basic-Seven-Step-Repair-System For Complete Wellness
Rheumatism (See Arthritis)	Victim Mentality	Emotional Balancing
	Lack of Love for Self & Others	Yin/Yang Balancing. Inner Child (3-5x 3 mo apart) Compassion (simultaneous w/each repair) Love (simultaneous w/each repair)
	Bacteria or Virus (Ankylosing Spondylitis)	Virus Neutralization (10x) Cellular Release (3x)
	Bones Fusing Together	Chiropractic Adjustment (regularly) Peanut Oil Spinal Massage (weekly or bi-weekly)
	Genetic Factors	DNA Repair (genetic) (3x)
	Broken Crystals	Crystal Repair
	Unresolved Karma	Karma Transmutation (20x 1x mo) Hot Epsom/Mineral Salt Baths Linolenic Acid Oleic Acid Diet Lacking Starches

Problem	Probable Cause	Probable Repairs & Techniques Needed To Resolve the Problem
	Lack of Exercise	Eight Glasses of Water With A Little Juice in It (daily) Crab Apple Bach Flower Remedy Ginger Tea Tai-Chi, Qigong, Yoga, Pilates, Walk Swimming, Physical Therapy Basic-Seven-Step-Repair-System For Complete Wellness
Right Side of Body Challenges	Masculine, Yang Aggressive, Giving Out Energy, Physical Plane Outdated Programs Karma	Yin/Yang Balancing Emotional Balancing Inner Child (3-5x 3 mo apart) Cookie & Scan Disc (10x 1 mo apart) Karma Transmutation (10x) Basic-Seven-Step-Repair-System For Complete Wellness
Left Side of Body Challenges	Feminine, Yin Spiritual Plane, Receiving Energy Outdated Programs Unresolved Karma	Yin/Yang Balancing Emotional Balancing Inner Child (3-5x, 1 mo apart) Cookie & Scan Disc (10x 1 mo apart) Karma Transmutation (10x) Basic-Seven-Step-Repair-System For Complete Wellness
Reiter's Disease	See Psoriasis/Arthritis Rheumatism	
Sciatica	Fear Relating To Finances Broken Grids Meridian Block/Break Misaligned Vertebrae Broken Crystals Tension, Stress Poor Posture	Inner Child (3-5x 3 mo apart) Yin/Yang Balancing Grid Repair Meridian Repair Chiropractic Adjustment Crystal Repair Stress Reduction (regularly) Massage, Tai-Chi, Yoga Standing Straight & Tall Core Body Exercise Basic-Seven-Step-Repair-System For Complete Wellness
Salivary Gland Challenges	Fear of Following through on Your Ideas Broken Grids Meridian Block/Break	Emotional Balancing Yin/Yang Balancing Inner Child (3-5x 3 mo apart) Grid Repair Meridian Repair

106

Problem	Probable Cause	Probable Repairs & Techniques Needed To Resolve the Problem
	TMJ	See Dentist
	Broken Crystals	Crystal Repair
		Heat to Area
		Lemon Drops
		Basic-Seven-Step-Repair-System For Complete Wellness
Shingles	Fearful of Future	Emotional Balancing
		Yin/Yang Balancing
		Inner Child (3-5x 3 mo apart)
	Herpes Virus	L-Lysine (500 mg daily)
	Chicken Pox Virus	Virus Neutralization (10x)
		Cellular Release (3x)
		Sea Salt Baths (2 cups)
		Basic-Seven-Step-Repair-System For Complete Wellness
Shoulder Challenges	Carrying World on Shoulders	Emotional Balancing
		Yin/Yang Balancing
		Inner Child (3-5x 3 mo apart)
	Broken Grids	Grid Repair
	Meridian Block/Break	Meridian Repair
	Misaligned Vertebrae	Chiropractic Adjustment
	Broken Crystals	Crystal Repair
	Tension, Stress	Stress Reduction (regularly)
		Massage, Tai-Chi, Yoga
	Poor Posture	Standing Straight & Tall
		Core Body Exercise, Pilates
		Basic-Seven-Step-Repair-System For Complete Wellness
Seizures	Mentally, Emotionally Escaping Life Challenges	Emotional Balancing
		Yin/Yang Balancing
	Feeling Overwhelmed by Responsibility	Inner Child (3-5x 3 mo apart)
		Elm Bach Flower Remedy
	Feelings of Persecution	
	Broken Grids Disrupting Electrical Signals in Brain	Grid Repair (10x)
	Broken Meridians (GV, CV, Possibly Gallbladder)	Meridian Repair
	Broken Crystals	Crystal Repair
	Electromagnetic Wounds	Wound Sealing
		Health Program
		Basic-Seven-Step-Repair-System For Complete Wellness

Problem	Probable Cause	Probable Repairs & Techniques Needed To Resolve the Problem
Sinus Problems (See Post Nasal Drip)	Lacking Self-Esteem Feeling Unloved	Love (simultaneous w/each repair) Emotional Balancing Inner Child (3-5x 3 mo apart) Yin/Yang Balancing Local Honey (1-3 tbsp daily)
	Meridian Block/Break Broken Grids Blocked Occipital, 3rd eye & Throat Chakra Allergies or Food Intolerances	Meridian Repair Grid Repair Chakra Balancing (Eat Right For Your Blood Type) by Dr. D'Amato Basic-Seven-Step-Repair-System For Complete Wellness
Skin Problems (See Psoriasis, Rashes, Hives)`	What is Under Your Skin? Nervous & Anxious Allergies Food Intolerances	Emotional Balancing Yin/Yang Balancing Inner Child (3-5x 3 mo apart) See Allergist (Eat Right For Your Blood Type) by Dr. D'Amato Sea Salt Baths (2 cups, 20 min) Stress Reduction Exercises Such As Yoga, Tai-Chi, Qigong Basic-Seven-Step-Repair-System For Complete Wellness
Slipped Disc	Feeling Alone Lack of Support Misaligned Vertebrae Broken Crystals in Spine Meridian Block/Break Electromagnetic Wounds Spine Damage	Emotional Balancing Yin/Yang Balancing Inner Child (3-5x 3 mo apart) Chiropractic Adjustment Crystal Repair Meridian Repair Wound Repair Health Program Spinal Repair Basic-Seven-Step-Repair-System For Complete Wellness
Snoring	Not Loving Self Locked into Old Programs Unresolved Karma Deviated Septum Sleep Apnea Heavy Drinking	Emotional Balancing Yin/Yang Balancing Inner Child (3-5x 3 mo apart Cookie & Scan Disc (10x 1x mo) Karma Transmutation (10x 1x mo) See Surgeon See Sleep Clinic Maximum One Drink (daily)

Problem	Probable Cause	Probable Repairs & Techniques Needed To Resolve the Problem
	Improper Diet for Blood Type Allergies or Food Intolerances	(Eat Right For Your Blood Type) by Dr. D'Amato
	Broken Crystals	Crystal Repair Basic-Seven-Step-Repair-System For Complete Wellness
Sore Throat	What Are You Not Saying? Emotions Unexpressed or Blocked	Chakra Balancing (throat) Emotional Balancing Yin/Yang Balancing Inner Child (3-5x 3 mo apart)
	Virus	Virus Neutralization (1x) Cellular Release (1x)
	Low Immune System	Thymus Chakra (tap gently) Proper Nutrition & Sleep (8-10 hrs) Sun & Exercise (daily) Mouth Rinse of 1 oz Hydrogen Peroxide & 3 oz Water (2x daily) Vitamin C (1,000-1,500 mg for Sore Throat) Chicken Soup Basic-Seven-Step-Repair-System For Complete Wellness
Spasms	Muscle Tension from Fear	Emotional Balancing Yin/Yang Balancing Inner Child (3-5x 3 mo apart)
	Outdated Programming	Cookie & Scan Disc (10x) Stress Reducing Exercises Such As Yoga, Tai-Chi, Meditation
	Overextension of Muscle Group	Ice (20 min), then Heat, Rest (until resolved) Massage (regularly) Trigger Point Injections for Pain Basic-Seven-Step-Repair-System For Complete Wellness
Spastic Colitis (See Arthritis)	Fear, Anxiety, Insecurity	Emotional Balancing Yin/Yang Balancing Inner Child (3-5x 3 mo apart)
	Outdated Programming Improper Diet Food Intolerances	Cookie & Scan Disc (10x) (Eat Right For Your Blood Type) by Dr. D'Amato Stress Reduction Exercises Such As Yoga, Tai-Chi, Qigong, Meditation Basic-Seven-Step-Repair-System

Problem	Probable Cause	Probable Repairs & Techniques Needed To Resolve the Problem
		For Complete Wellness
Spleen Challenges	Lack of Love for Self & Others	Love Tech(simultaneous w/all repairs)
	Lack of Emotional Balance	Emotional Balancing
	Intense Negative Feelings	Yin/Yang Balancing
		Inner Child (3-5x 3 mo apart)
	Meridian Block/Break	Meridian Repair
	Blocked Chakras	Chakra Balancing
		Virus Neutralization (3x)
		Cellular Release(3x 3 mo apart)
	Unresolved Karma	Karma Transmutation (10x)
		Basic-Seven-Step-Repair-System For Complete Wellness
Sprains	Difficulty Making Changes	Emotional Balancing
	Outdated Programming	Cookie & Scan Disc (10x)
	Karma	Karma Transmutation (10x 1 mo apart)
		Emotional Balancing
		Yin/Yang Balancing
		Inner Child (3-5x 3 mo apart)
		Ice (20 min), then Heat
	Overextension of Abilities	Pacing Yourself
	Hormonal Imbalance (Women)	See Endocrinologist & Anti-Aging Specialist
	Chemical Imbalance	Chemical Balancing
		Basic-Seven-Step-Repair-System For Complete Wellness
Sterility	Fear, Not Feeling Safe on a Soul Level	Inner Child (3-5x 3 mo apart)
		Emotional Balancing
	Choosing Not to Have Children in This Life	Yin/Yang Balancing
	Wearing Briefs (Men)	Wear Boxer Shorts
	Blocked Sacral & Root Chakras	Chakra Balancing
	Meridian Block/Break	Meridian Repair
	Outdated Programming	Cookie & Scan Disc (10x 1x mo)
	Karma	Karma Transmutation (10-20x 1x mo)
	Hormonal Imbalance	See Endocrinologist & Anti-Aging Specialist
	Cords	Cord Cutting
		Basic-Seven-Step-Repair-System For Complete Wellness
Spurs	Ongoing Resentment	Forgiveness Technique (10-20x)

110

Problem	Probable Cause	Probable Repairs & Techniques Needed To Resolve the Problem
Spine (See Arthritis)		Emotional Balancing Inner Child (3-5x 3 mo apart) Yin/Yang Balancing
	Broken Crystals	Crystal Repair
	Meridian Block/Break	Meridian Repair
	For Pain	Trigger Point Injections (monthly) Peanut Oil Spinal Massage
	Lack of Exercise	Stretching and Other Exercises for Agility Such As Yoga, Tai-Chi, Qigong, etc.
	Poor Posture	Standing Straight & Tall Basic-Seven-Step-Repair-System For Complete Wellness
Stiff Neck	Inflexibility in Attitude Unable to See Others' Opinions	Cookie & Scan Disc (10x) Inner Child (3-5x 3 mo apart) Emotional Balancing Yin/Yang Balancing
	Broken Crystals Misaligned Vertebrae	Crystal Repair Chiropractic Adjustment Sleeping In A Drafty Place Stretching Exercises Such As Yoga Tai-Chi, Qigong, etc.
	Poor Posture	Standing Straight & Tall Basic-Seven-Step-Repair-System For Complete Wellness
Stiffness	Inflexibility In Attitude Unable To See Others Opinions	Cookie & Scan Disc (10x 1x mo) Inner Child (3-5x 3 mo apart) Emotional Balancing Yin/Yang Balancing
	Broken Crystals Misaligned Vertebrae	Crystal Repair Chiropractic Adjustment Avoid Sleeping In A Draft Stretching Exercises-Yoga Tai-Chi, Qigong, etc.
	Poor Posture	Standing Straight & Tall Basic-Seven-Step-Repair-System For Complete Wellness
Stomach Challenges (See Heartburn, Gastritis, Ulcers)	Fear, Nerves	Emotional Balancing Yin/Yang Balancing Inner Child (3-5x 3 mo apart) Stress Reduction Exercises Such As Yoga, Tai-Chi, Qigong, Meditation
	Meridian Block/Break	Meridian Repair (5x)

Problem	Probable Cause	Probable Repairs & Techniques Needed To Resolve the Problem
	(Especially Women with C-section or Hysterectomy)	
	Broken Grids	Grid Repair
	Solar Plexus Chakra	Chakra Balancing
	Misaligned Vertebrae	Chiropractic Adjustment
	Cords Around Intestines	Cord Cutting
	Improper Diet	(Eat Right For Your Blood Type)
	Food Intolerances	by Dr. D'Amato
	Acidic Diet	Alkaline, Plant Based Diet
	H. Pylori Bacteria	Antibiotic (see doctor)
	Causes Ulcers	Virus Neutralization (3x)
		Cellular Release (1x)
		DNA Repair
		Basic-Seven-Step-Repair-System For Complete Wellness
Stroke (Cerebrovascular)	Feeling Overwhelmed	Emotional Balancing
	Kick the Bucket Rather Than Change ~ Stress, Lack of Joy	Yin/Yang Balancing
		Inner Child (3-5x 3 mo apart)
		Stress Reduction Exercises Such As Yoga, Tai-Chi, Qigong, Meditation
	Plague, Cholesterol Clogging Veins	Cardiac Repair (10-12x ASAP)
	Acidic Diet	Alkaline Diet Is Key
	Meridian Block/Break	Meridian Repair
	Chakra Blocks	Chakra Balancing
		Basic-Seven-Step-Repair-System For Complete Wellness
Stuttering	Emotionally Insecure	Emotional Balancing
	Inner Child Crying	Inner Child (3-5x 3 mo apart)
		Yin/Yang Balancing
		Speech Therapy
		Basic-Seven-Step-Repair-System For Complete Wellness
Sty	Unresolved Anger	Emotional Balancing
		Yin/Yang Balancing
		Inner Child (3-5x 3 mo apart)
	Virus	Virus Neutralization (3x)
		Cellular Release (1x)
		Basic-Seven-Step-Repair-System For Complete Wellness
Suicide or Suicidal	Feeling Hopeless	Emotional Balancing
		Yin/Yang Balancing

Problem	Probable Cause	Probable Repairs & Techniques Needed To Resolve the Problem
		Inner Child (3-5x 3mo apart)
	Possible Entity Possession	Entity Removal
	Stuck in That Crazy Place	Cookie & Scan Disc (10x 1 mo apart)
	Karma	Karma Transmutation (10-20x 1x mo)
	Lack of Serotonin	Sun Exposure (15 min-1 hour daily)
	Chemical Imbalance	Chemical Balancing
	Unbalanced Crown Chakra	Chakra Balancing
		Grid Repair
	Chronic Depression	Psychiatric Care & Medicine
	Lack of Love & Joy	Love (simultaneous w/each repair)
	Possible Drug/Alcohol Addiction	Rehabilitation Facility
	Blueprint Imbalance	Blueprint Restoration
		Basic-Seven-Step-Repair-System For Complete Wellness
Swelling (Edema, Holding Fluids)	Stuck in Mental, Emotional Patterns	Emotional Balancing
	Outdated Programs	Cookie & Scan Disc (10x 1x mo)
	Karma	Karma Transmutation
		Yin/Yang Balancing
		Inner Child (3-5x)
	Meridian Block/Break	Meridian Repair
	Blocks in Chakras	Chakra Balancing
	Broken Grids	Grid Repair
	Toxic Lymph System	Lymphatic Technique (5x)
	Lack of Exercise	Qigong, Tai-Chi, Bike, Walk
	Improper Diet	(Eat Right For Your Blood Type)
	Food Intolerances	by Dr. D'Amato
	Cords Strangling Heart	Cord Cutting
	Total Body Energetically Blocked	Striking I & II
		Basic-Seven-Step-Repair-System For Complete Wellness
Teeth (See Jaw)	Hard Time Breaking Down New Thoughts & Concepts In Moving Forward With Change	Emotional Balancing
		Yin/Yang Balancing
		Inner Child (3-5x 3 mo apart)
	Not Maintaining Teeth	See Dentist (regularly)
	Possible Effect of Accident	See Dentist
	TMJ	Caffeine Reduction
	Stress	Stress Reduction Exercises Such As Yoga, Tai-Chi, Qigong, Meditation
	Misaligned Vertebrae	Chiropractic Adjustments
		Basic-Seven-Step-Repair-System

Problem	Probable Cause	Probable Repairs & Techniques Needed To Resolve the Problem
		For Complete Wellness
Temporomandibular Joint (TMJ)	See Teeth & Jaw	
Throat	See Sore Throat	
Thighs	Fear of Change	Emotional Balancing Yin/Yang Balancing Inner Child (3-5x 3 mo apart)
	Outdated Programs	Cookie & Scan Disc (10x 1x mo)
	Karma	Karma Transmutation (10x 1x mo)
	Lack of Exercise	Walk, Bike Basic-Seven-Step-Repair-System For Complete Wellness
Thrush	Unresolved Anger over Personal Decisions	Emotional Balancing Yin/Yang Balancing Inner Child (3-5x 3 mo apart)
	Outdated Programs	Cookie & Scan Disc (10x 1x mo)
	Karma	Karma Transmutation (10x 1x mo)
	Carb & Sugar Diet	Complex Carb, Protein, Veggie, Fruit Diet
	Improper Diet	(Eat Right For Your Blood Type) by Dr. D'Amato
	Yeast Infection	Yogurt W/Live Cultures Essential Enzymes or Probiotics Basic-Seven-Step-Repair-System For Complete Wellness
Thymus (Higher Heart)	Fear, Feeling Persecuted With No Protection	Emotional Balancing Yin/Yang Balancing Inner Child (3-5x 3 mo apart)
	Low Immune System	Good Nutrition Sleep (8-10 hrs daily) Daily Sun Exposure
	High Stress Levels	Stress Reduction Exercises Such As Yoga, Tai-Chi, Qigong, Meditation
	Meridian Block/Break	Meridian Repair
	Thymus Chakra Blocked	Chakra Balancing Love (simultaneous w/each repair) Thymus Chakra (tap gently) Basic-Seven-Step-Repair-System For Complete Wellness
Thyroid	See Hypo & Hyper Thyroidism	

Problem	Probable Cause	Probable Repairs & Techniques Needed To Resolve the Problem
Tics, Twitches	Fear, Nervous	Emotional Balancing Yin/Yang Balancing Inner Child (3-5x 3 mo apart)
	Too Much Caffeine or Other Stimulant	Caffeine Reduction
	Outdated Programs	Cookie & Scan Disc (10x 1x mo)
	Karma	Karma Transmutation (10x 1x mo) Basic-Seven-Step-Repair-System For Complete Wellness
Tinnitus	What Don't You Want to Hear?	Emotional Balancing
	Rigidity in Opinions	Yin/Yang Balancing Inner Child (3-5x 3 mo apart)
	Outdated Programs	Cookie & Scan Disc (10x 1x mo)
	Cords	Cord Cutting
	Ear Chakra Blocked	Chakra Balancing
	Inner Ear Infection	See Doctor Virus Neutralization (3x) Cellular Release (1x)
	Karma	Karma Transmutation (10-20x 1x mo)
	Cell Phone Use	Cell Phone Use Cessation Homeopathic Radiation Remedy Basic-Seven-Step-Repair-System For Complete Wellness
Toes Challenges	Feet Represent Moving Forward, Toes Represent Worrying About Moving Forward.	Emotional Balancing Yin/Yang Balancing Inner Child (3-5x 3 mo apart)
	Meridian Block/Break	Meridian Repair
	Chakra Blocks In Toes	Chakra Balancing
	Broken Grids	Grid Repair Basic-Seven-Step-Repair-System For Complete Wellness
Tonsillitis	Fear, Unbalanced Emotions	Emotional Balancing Yin/Yang Balancing Inner Child (3-5x 3 mo apart)
	Meridian Breaks in CV, GV or Throat	Meridian Repair
	Blocked Lymphatic System	Lymph Technique (3x) Virus Neutralization Cellular Release (1x)
	Blocked Throat Chakra	Chakra Balancing

Problem	Probable Cause	Probable Repairs & Techniques Needed To Resolve the Problem
		Basic-Seven-Step-Repair-System For Complete Wellness
Tuberculosis	Unbalanced Emotions Obsessed With Self	Emotional Balancing Yin/Yang Balancing Inner Child (3-5x 3 mo apart)
	Outdated Programs For Infection	Cookie & Scan Disc (10x 1x mo) Antibiotics Virus Neutralization (10x) Cellular Release (3x 3 mo apart)
	Meridian Block/Break Genetic	Meridian Repair DNA-(5x) Repair Basic-Seven-Step-Repair-System For Complete Wellness
Tumors	Lumps of Unforgiveness, Hatred, Jealousy, Anger & Hurts	Forgiveness Technique (15x) Emotional Balancing Yin/Yang Balancing Inner Child (3-5x 3 mo apart)
	Blocked Lymphatic System Acidic Diet Resulting in Latent Tissue Acidosis Outdated Programs Unresolved Karma	Lymph Repair (4x) Alkaline Diet Is Key Cookie & Scan Disc (10x 1x mo) Karma Transmutation (10x 1x mo) Energetic System Scan for Blocks Basic-Seven-Step-Repair-System For Complete Wellness
Ulcerative Colitis	See Psoriasis & Arthritis	
Ulcers	Poor Self-Esteem, Feelings of Unworthiness	Inner Child (3-5x 3 mo apart) Yin/Yang Balancing Emotional Balancing Love (simultaneous w/each repair)
	Unbalanced Blueprint Outdated Programs H. Pylori Virus	Blueprint Restoration Cookie & Scan Disc (10x) Antibiotics (see doctor) Virus Neutralization (10x) Cellular Release (3x)
	Poor Dental Hygiene	Brushing & Flossing (2x daily) Mouthwash or Mix With Hydrogen Peroxide Dental Visits (regularly)
	Meridian Block/Break Karma Acidic Diet	Meridian Repair Karma Transmutation (10x) Alkaline, Plant Based Diet

Problem	Probable Cause	Probable Repairs & Techniques Needed To Resolve the Problem
	Blocked Solar Plexus Food Intolerances	Chakra Balancing (Eat Right For Your Blood Type) by Dr. D'Amato Basic-Seven-Step-Repair-System For Complete Wellness
Urinary Infections	Having A Blame Mentality Needs To Grow Up & Take Responsibility for Life Path Outdated Programs Lack of Forgiveness Unresolved Karma	Inner Child (3-5x) Emotional Balancing Yin/Yang Balancing Cookie & Scan Disc (10x) Forgiveness (10x) Unresolved Karma Transmutation (10x) Antibiotics (see doctor) Virus Neutralization Cellular Release Organic Cranberry Juice
	Meridian Block/Break Blocked Sacral Chakra	Meridian Repair Chakra Balancing Basic-Seven-Step-Repair-System For Complete Wellness
Vaginitis	Subconsciously Rejects Sex Over Anger or Guilt Outdated Programs High Carbohydrate Diet Unresolved Karma Meridian Block/Break Blocked Root Chakra	Inner Child (3-5x 3 mo apart) Emotional Balancing Yin/Yang Balancing Cookie & Scan Disc (10x) High Protein, Veggie, Fruit Diet Yogurt With Live Cultures Monistat Cream (follow directions) Karma Transmutation (10x 1x mo) Meridian Repair Chakra Balancing Basic-Seven-Step-Repair-System For Complete Wellness
Vertigo	Emotional Imbalance Drifting, Resignation Apathy Demorpheous Inner Ear Infection Wax in Ear Possible Heart Issues Possible Vein Issues (See Cholesterol) Total Exhaustion Dehydration	Emotional Balancing Inner Child Yin/Yang Balancing Removal See Specialist Ear Candling Cardiac Technique (12x) Alkaline Diet Is Key Rest Plenty of Fluids

Problem	Probable Cause	Probable Repairs & Techniques Needed To Resolve the Problem
	Blocked Crown/3ʳᵈ Eye	Chakra Balancing
	Misaligned Vertebrae	Chiropractic Adjustment
		Basic-Seven-Step-Repair-System For Complete Wellness
Viral Infection	Lack of Joy	Forgiveness Technique (10x)
	Outdated Programs	Cookie & Scan Disc (10x 1x mo)
		Emotional Balancing
		Yin/Yang Balancing
		Inner Child (3-5x 3 mo apart)
	Virus	Virus Neutralization (3x)
		Cellular Release (1x)
		Love Technique w/each Repair
	Acidic Diet	Alkaline Diet
	Low Immune System	Good Nutrition, Rest, Exercise
		Thymus Chakra (tap gently)
		Basic-Seven-Step-Repair-System For Complete Wellness
Vomiting	Fear	Emotional Balancing
		Yin/Yang Balancing
		Inner Child (3-5x 3 mo apart)
	Food Poisoning	Natural Processing of Poison
		See Doctor
	Acidic Diet	Alkaline Diet
	Improper Diet	Eat Right For Your Blood Type by Dr. D'Amato
	Gallbladder Challenge	Meridian Repair
	Gallstones	Esoteric Surgery to Remove Stones
	Parasites	Holistic Remedy for Parasites
		Basic-Seven-Step-Repair-System For Complete Wellness
Wrists	Imbalanced Yin/Yang	Yin/Yang Balancing
		Emotional Balancing
		Inner Child (3-5x 3 mo apart)
	Meridian Block/Break	Meridian Repair
	Blocked Wrist Chakra	Chakra Balancing
	Overextension of Repetitive Motion, e.g. Computer	Carpal Tunnel Syndrome Repetitive Motion Cessation
	Wrist Out Of Alignment	Chiropractic Adjustment
		EFA's
		Multi B Complex
		Basic-Seven-Step-Repair-System For Complete Wellness

Problem	Probable Cause	Probable Repairs & Techniques Needed To Resolve the Problem
Yeast Infection	Not Owning Own Power	Yin/Yang Balancing
	Not Supplying Own Needs	Emotional Balancing
		Inner Child (3-5x 3 mo apart)
	Outdated Programs	Cookie & Scan Disc (10x 1x mo)
	Unresolved Karma	Karma Transmutation (10x 1x mo)
	Imbalanced Blueprint	Blueprint Restoration
	Meridian Block/Break	Meridian Repair
	Blocked Root Chakra	Chakra Balancing
	Carb & Sugar Diet	Complex Carb, Protein, Veggie, Fruit Diet
	Improper Diet	(Eat Right For Your Blood Type) by Dr. D'Amato
		Yogurt With Live Cultures
		Essential Enzymes or Probiotics
		Basic-Seven-Step-Repair-System For Complete Wellness

Now that you have had a chance to look through the alphabetized itemized lists in The Manual, you will no doubt see that repairing the Physical Body through the Electromagnetic Body can get complicated. However, there are many different modalities that Energy Medicine Practitioners have learned in various Energy Medicine Workshops that they will recognize here, such as:

Energetic Hygiene
Grid Repair
Chakra Balancing
Prana Tube Filling
Meridian Repair
DNA Repair
Karma Transmutation

The challenge that most Energy Medicine Practitioners run up against is that they have learned different techniques piecemeal, and cannot see how to put all the pieces together to perform a cohesive miraculous healing. However, by utilizing this book, it will be easy to put all of the pieces together. The Manual weaves together all of the energetic techniques necessary to form a complete tapestry for the healing of the Electromagnetic Body. My suggestion for Energy Medicine Practitioners is to try every technique for which you have been trained and add in the practical suggestions. In this way, you and your loved ones and clients will gain much benefit.

However, some of the intermediate and advanced techniques are unique to the YATUVAY modality. These were given by The Father to Adolphina Shephard for the benefit of humanity. Those of you who are already Energy Medicine Practitioners may want to consider taking YATUVAY workshops to upgrade your knowledge, so that you may become a true master at transforming The Electromagnetic Body, therefore, the Physical, Emotional and Mental Bodies as well.

For those of you who are novices, you can start your education in Energy Medicine by taking YATUVAY Workshops. This is actually a benefit to a beginner, in that you do not have to unlearn other practices or techniques that are not compatible with YATUVAY methods. YATUVAY administers Laying-On-Of-The-Hands, prayers, distance healing and esoteric tools, utilizing "The Power of One" to facilitate YATUVAY'S Energy Medicine healing sessions. Listed below are some of the healing methods that are unique to YATUVAY.

The Fountain of Youth Series

Striking I
Striking II
Charging the Batteries
Repairing the Endocrine System
Filling Your Gas Tank
Facelifts

Repairing the Emotional & Mental Bodies

Blueprint Restoration
Chemical Balancing
Healing the Inner Child
Compassion Technique
Yin/Yang Balancing
Emotional & Mental Balancing

Charging the Emotional & Mental Reserves
Activating the Keys of Abundance Consciousness

<u>Repairing the Physical Body through the Electromagnetic Body</u>

Blueprint Restoration
Repairing Total Body DNA
Total Body Lymphatic Cleansing
Cardiac Repair Technique
Virus/Bacteria Neutralization
Total Body Cellular Release
Chemical Balancing
Spinal Repair
Crystal System Repair
Repairing and/or Replacing the Etheric Organs
Esoteric Surgery

<u>Energetic Hygiene</u>

Energetic Hygiene Technique
Using Filters
Closing Wormholes, Vortexes, Portals
Cookie and Scan Disc

My suggestion for Energy Medicine Practitioners is to use the Basic-Seven-Step-Repair-System along with the practical suggestions. Then try every technique for which you have been trained in previous energy classes, modifying and incorporating YATUVAY methods into these varied techniques. In this way, you, your loved ones, and your clients will gain much benefit.

To find out when and where YATUVAY Workshops are being held, please go to Adolphina's website at www.AdolphinaShephard.com or email Adolphina at AdolphinaShephard@msn.com.

If you wish to facilitate a YATUVAY Workshop or Seminar, please email Adolphina.

To schedule a YATUVAY healing session, please go to Adolphina's website to see a list of YATUVAY Practitioners in your area. If you wish, you may subscribe to Adolphina's website to get updates on workshops, updated news and to sign up for the YATUVAY newsletter.